ONE MINUTE PLEASE

CONTENTS

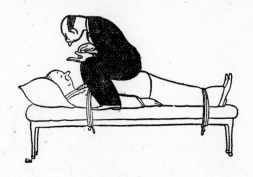

First published in Great Britain,
September, 1945
Second impression October, 1945
Third impression December, 1945

All rights reserved

PRINTED IN GREAT BRITAIN
by GIBBS, BAMFORTH (LUTON) LTD.
THE LEAGRAVE PRESS, LUTON
in 10-point Garamond type, leaded.

A2730

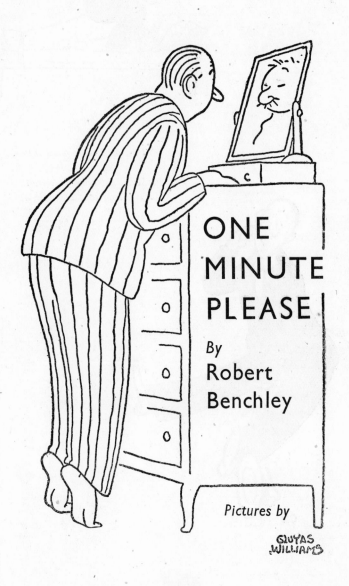

ONE MINUTE PLEASE

By
Robert Benchley

Pictures by

GLUYAS
WILLIAMS

DENNIS DOBSON LTD.
29, GREAT QUEEN STREET LONDON, W.C.2

"One Minute, Please!"

I AM known as a bad business man from one end of the country to just a little beyond the same end. Practically every one in my class in kindergarten went into business after graduation, and when I say business I mean business. Whenever I see them now they are always dressed up in stiff shirts and are making marks on the backs of envelopes. Get me a hundred of my old schoolmates together and let them talk from 9 a.m. until almost dinner time and I won't understand a word they are saying. It is only around dinner time that I begin to catch a glimmer of sense and then they have to come right out and say " Martini " or " Green turtle soup." At this point I join the party.

But not until I have had it said to me eight or a dozen times that I ought to be more businesslike. " Good old Bob," they say (those of them who remember that my name is " Bob "), " you are just a sucker to be so impractical. Why don't you let us take some of your money and triple it for you ? "

Leaving aside the question " What money ? " I am frankly at a loss for something to say. Here I am, just a dreamer, and there they are, captains of industry, or, at any rate, second lieutenants. They have the advantage of me.

Of course, if I wanted to, I might point out that out of a possible $5000 which I have made since I left school I have had $3000 worth of good food (all of which has gone into making bone and muscle and some nice fat), $1500 worth of theatre tickets, and $500 worth of candy ; whereas many of my business friends have simply had $5000 worth of whatever that stock was which got so yellow along about last November.

I was sympathetic with all the boys at that time and even advanced a little cash in a sparing manner, but I couldn't help remembering the days during the summer when I had to sit and listen to them say : " Well, I made $650,000 over the week-end. What will you have, Bob, old man ? " And all the time I was, in my old impractical way, sinking my money into silk neckties (which I still have) and throwing it away on life-giving beefsteaks.

I do not intend to dwell on this phase of life's whirligig, however. Who can tell, perhaps some day even we spendthrifts may find ourselves short of cash. In the meantime, those of us who have nothing but fripperies to show for our money have had a good laugh. At least we've got the fripperies.

What I do want to dwell on is the point that there are still a great many practices which are considered businesslike and efficient and which any one of us old dreamers could improve upon and speed up. Now you sit still and read this. I have sat still and listened to you long enough.

First, there is the question of business telephoning. During the last five or six years there has spread throughout the business world a method of telephoning which, so far as I am concerned, bids fair to destroy all channels of business communication. If it keeps up, I, for one, will go back to the old Indian runner and carrier pigeon methods. I won't stand for this another day. In fact, I stopped standing for it a year ago.

I refer to the delayed pass play, so popular among busy executives. In this play your busy executive, when he wants to get me on the telephone (why he should want to get me on the telephone is a mystery), says to his secretary : " Get me Mr. Benchley on the wire, Miss Whatney." You see, he hasn't got the time to get me himself, what with all those stocks he has to tend to ; so he has Miss Whatney do it for him. So far, pretty good ! Miss Whatney looks up my number in the book and gives it to the operator at the switchboard, thereby releasing the busy executive for other duties, such as biting off the end of a cigar or drawing circles on his scratch pad.

The scene now changes and we see me, the impractical dreamer, sitting at an old typewriter with nothing to do but finish an article which was due the day before. My telephone rings and I, in my slipshod, impractical way, answer it. And what do I get for my pains ?

" Is this Vanderbilt 0647 ? Is Mr. Benchley there ? Just a minute, please ! "

Having nothing to do but wool-gather, I wait. In about two minutes I hear another female voice saying : " Is this Mr. Benchley ? Just a minute, please, Mr. Kleek wants to speak to you."

Remember, it is Mr. Kleek who is calling *me* up. I don't want to speak to Mr. Kleek. I wouldn't care if I never spoke to him. In fact, I am not sure that I know who Mr. Kleek is.

" Just a minute, please," comes the voice again. " Mr. Kleek is talking on another wire."

Now, fascinating as this information is, it really wasn't worth getting up out of my chair for. Mr. Kleek could be busy on eight other wires and my life would go on just about the same. Am I to be called away from my work to be told that a Mr. Kleek is talking on another wire ? I think this out as I stand there waiting.

Finally, after several minutes, I hear a man's voice.

" Hello," it says gruffly : " who is this ? " I am not only to be told to wait until Mr. Kleek is ready to speak to me, but I am to be treated by Mr. Kleek as if I had infringed on his time. At this point I frankly flare up.

" Who is this yourself ? " I snarl. " This was your idea, not mine ! "

Then evidently Miss Whatney tells Mr. Kleek that she has got Mr. Benchley on the wire, and he is somewhat mollified. But I want to tell you, Mr. Kleek, that by that time I am not on the wire any longer and you can stick that telephone ear-piece into the side of your head. Furthermore, from now on, the minute I am called to the telephone and told to wait a minute, that Mr. Anybody wants

8

to speak to me, I hang up so quickly that the hook drops off. If Mr. Kleek or any other busy executive wants to speak to me he can be there within four seconds after I answer or he can put in the call again. I may be just an old wool-gatherer, but I want to gather my wool somewhere else than at a telephone receiver.

It is possible that the telephone has been responsible for more business inefficiency than any other agency except laudanum. It has such an air of pseudo-efficiency about it that people feel efficient the minute they take the receiver off the hook. A business man could be talking with Ajax, the mechanical chess player, on the other end of the wire and still feel he was getting somewhere, simply because to any one passing the door he looks as if he were very busy. There is something about saying " O.K." and hanging up the receiver with a bang that kids a man into feeling that he has just pulled off a big deal, even if he has only called up Central to find out the correct time. For this reason business men use the telephone exclusively when almost any other form of communication would be quicker.

In the old days when you wanted to get in touch with a man you wrote a note, sprinkled it with sand, and gave it to a man on horse-back. It probably was delivered within half an hour, depending on how big a lunch the horse had had. But in these busy days of rush-rush-rush, it sometimes is a week before you can catch your man on the telephone. The call is put in, but he is out. You tell your secretary to keep calling, but, if the man takes any kind of care of himself at all, he is out most all day in the fresh air. So day after day the secretary keeps calling and, in this way, autumn turns into winter and winter to spring. Perhaps you never get him.

A busy executive said to me the other day in an exasperated tone : " Aren't you ever in ? I have been trying to get you on the telephone for five days. What do you do with your time, cut lawns ? " You see, I am the one who was in the wrong. I was the impractical one.

I might have told him about that new invention called the " type-writer," whereby, if you can't get a man on the telephone, you can drop him a note which will reach him the next morning. Or I also might have told him that I was in my office all the time, but was so busy working that I had left word with the telephone operator not to bother me with time-wasting calls from business men. In either case, dropping me a note would have saved him four days of tele-phoning. But apparently note-dropping is considered a relic of Civil War days and is not to be considered in the bustle of modern business. You must use the telephone, even if it doesn't get you anywhere.

The telephone is the particular pet of the go-getter who won't take no for an answer. He has a passion for long-distance calls. Let us say that his organisation is getting up a dinner in Chicago and wants to get an after-dinner speaker from New York. The go-getter is, of course, chairman of the dinner committee because he gets things done. He guarantees to get the New York speaker. " Leave it to me," he says, knowingly. And, even as he says it, he is putting in a long-distance call for New York. Bingo—like that! The New York man answers and gets the following :

" This is Ferley of the Autumn Coat and Suit speaking! We're holding a dinner here on Feb. 10, and you're coming out to speak for us !—Oh, yes, you are ! I won't take ' no ' for an answer. . . . O, yes, you can—I'll call those people up and tell them you're coming to us. . . . Now, not another word !—See you on the 10th ! "

With this he hangs up and reports to the committee that he has the speaker sewed up. The fact that the New York man can't go to Chicago on the 10th and has no intention of going doesn't enter into the calculations at all. No one is supposed to be able to resist the man with the telephone personality. He sweeps everything before him.

The only drawback is that, two days before the dinner, when it is found out that the New York speaker meant what he said and really isn't coming, the go-getter has to go-get somebody through a local agency to do card tricks for the diners. " That's the trouble with dealing with these literary guys," he thunders. " You can't count on them ! " And he puts in another long-distance call just to quiet his nerves.

And so it goes through life. There are the doers and the dreamers, the men who make every second count and the men who waste their time with nothing to show for it. The first are the business men of the country, the others are the impractical fellows who write and draw pictures. Or perhaps it is just the other way 'round. I always get these things mixed.

Kiddie-Kar
Travel

IN America there are two classes of travel—first class, and with children. Travelling with children corresponds roughly to travelling third-class in Bulgaria. They tell me there is nothing lower in the world than third-class Bulgarian travel.

The actual physical discomfort of travelling with the Kiddies is not so great, although you do emerge from it looking as if you had just moved the piano upstairs single-handed. It is the mental wear-and-tear that tells and for a sensitive man there is only one thing worse, and that is a church wedding in which he is playing the leading comedy rôle.

There are several branches of the ordeal of Going on Choo-Choo, and it is difficult to tell which is the roughest. Those who have taken a very small baby on a train maintain that this ranks as pleasure along with having a nerve killed. On the other hand, those whose wee companions are in the romping stage, simply laugh at the claims of the first group. Sometimes you will find a man who has both an infant *and* a romper with him. Such a citizen should receive a salute of twenty-one guns every time he enters the city and should be allowed to wear the insignia of the Pater Dolorosa, giving him the right to solicit alms on the cathedral steps.

There is much to be said for those who maintain that rather should the race be allowed to die out than that babies should be taken from place to place along our national arteries' of traffic. On the other hand, there *are* moments when babies are asleep. (Oh, yes, there are. There *must* be.) But it is practically a straight run of ten or a dozen hours for your child of four. You may have a little trouble in getting the infant to doze off, especially as the train newsboy waits crouching in the vestibule until he sees signs of slumber on the child's face and then rushes in to yell, " Cop of *Life*, out to-day ! " right by its pink, shell-like ear. But after it *is* asleep, your troubles are over except for wondering how you can shift your ossifying arm to a new position without disturbing its precious burden.

If the child is of an age which denies the existence of sleep, however, preferring to run up and down the aisle of the car rather than sit in its chair (at least a baby can't get out of its chair unless it falls out and even then it can't go far), then every minute of the trip is full of fun. On the whole, having travelled with children of all the popular ages, I would be inclined to award the Hair-Shirt to the man who successfully completes the ride with a boy of, let us say, three.

In the first place, you start with the pronounced ill will of two-thirds of the rest of the occupants of the car. You see them as they

You start with the pronounced ill-will of the rest of the occupants.

come in, before the train starts, glancing at you and yours with little or no attempt to conceal the fact that they wish they had waited for the four o'clock. Across from you is perhaps a large man who, in his home town, has a reputation for eating little children. He wears a heavy gold watch chain and wants to read through a lot of reports on the trip. He is just about as glad to be opposite a small boy as he would be if it were a hurdy-gurdy.

In back of you is a lady in a black silk dress who doesn't like the porter. Ladies in black silk dresses always seem to board the train with an aversion to the porter. The fact that the porter has to be in the same car with her makes her fussy to start with, and when she discovers that in front of her is a child of three who is already eating (you simply have to give him a lemon drop to keep him quiet at least until the train starts), she decides that the best thing to do is simply to ignore him and not give him the slightest encouragement to become friendly. The child therefore picks her out immediately to be his buddy.

For a time after things get to going all you have to do is answer questions about the scenery. This is only what you must expect when you have children, and it happens no matter where you are. You can always say that you don't know who lives in that house or what that cow is doing. Sometimes you don't even have to look up when you say that you don't know. This part is comparatively easy.

It is when the migratory fit comes on that you will be put to the test. Suddenly you look and find the boy staggering down the aisle, peering into the faces of people as he passes them. " Here! Come back here, Roger! " you cry, lurching after him and landing across the knees of the young lady two seats down. Roger takes this as a signal for a game and starts to run, screaming with laughter. After four steps he falls and starts to cry.

On being carried kicking back to his seat, he is told that he mustn't run down the aisle again. This strikes even Roger as funny, because it is such a flat thing to say. Of course he is going to run down the aisle again and he knows it as well as you do. In the meantime, however, he is perfectly willing to spend a little time with the lady in the black silk dress.

" Here, Roger," you say, " don't bother the lady."

" Hello, little boy," the lady says, nervously, and tries to go back to her book. The interview is over as far as she is concerned. Roger, however, thinks that it would be just dandy to get up in her lap. This has to be stopped, and Roger has to be whispered to.

He then announces that it is about time that he went to the washroom. You march down the car, steering him by the shoulders and both lurching together as the train takes the curves and attracting wide attention to your very obvious excursion. Several kindly people smile knowingly at you as you pass and try to pat the boy on the head, but their advances are repelled, it being a rule of all children to look with disfavour on any attentions from strangers.

The only people they want to play with are those who hate children.

On reaching the wash-room you discover that the porter has just locked it and taken the key with him, simply to be nasty. This raises quite a problem. You explain the situation as well as possible, which turns out to be not well enough. There is every indication of loud crying and perhaps worse. You call attention to the Burrows Rustless Screen sign which you are just passing and stand in the passageway by the drinking cups, feverishly trying to find things in the landscape as it whirls by which will serve to take the mind off the tragedy of the moment. You become so engrossed in this important task that it is some time before you discover that you are completely blocking the passageway and the progress of some fifteen

Before you discover that you are completely blocking the passageway.

people who want to get off at Utica. There is nothing for you to do but head the procession and get off first.

Once out in the open, the pride and prop of your old age decides that the thing to do is pay the engineer a visit, and starts off up the platform at a terrific rate. This amuses the onlookers and gives you a little exercise after being cramped up in that old car all the morning. The imminent danger of the train's starting without you only adds to the fun. At that, there might be worse things than being left in Utica. One of them is getting back on the train again to face the old gentleman with the large watch chain.

The final phase of the ordeal, however, is still in store for you when you make your way (and Roger's way) into the diner. Here the plunging march down the aisle of the car is multiplied by six (the diner is never any nearer than six cars and usually is part of another train). On the way, Roger sees a box of animal crackers belonging to a little girl and commandeers it. The little girl, putting up a fight, is promptly pushed over, starting what promises to be a free-for-all fight between the two families. Lurching along after the apologies have been made, it is just a series of unwarranted attacks by Roger on sleeping travellers and equally unwarranted evasions by Roger of the kindly advances of very nice people who love children.

In the diner, it turns out that the nearest thing they have suited to Roger's customary diet is veal cutlets, and you hardly think that his mother would approve of those. Everything else has peppers or sardines in it. A curry of lamb across the way strikes the boy's fancy and he demands some of that. On being told that he has not the slightest chance in the world of getting it but how would he like a little crackers-and-milk, he becomes quite upset and threatens to throw a fork at the Episcopal clergyman sitting opposite. Pieces of toast are waved alluringly in front of him and he is asked to consider the advantages of preserved figs and cream, but it is curry of lamb or he gets off the train. He doesn't act like this at home. In fact, he is noted for his tractability. There seems to be something about the train that brings out all the worst that is in him, all the hidden traits that he has inherited from his mother's side of the family. There is nothing else to do but say firmly : " Very well, then, Roger. We'll go back *without* any nice dinner," and carry him protesting from the diner, apologising to the head steward for the scene and considering dropping him overboard as you pass through each vestibule.

In fact, I had a cousin once who had to take three of his little ones on an all-day trip from Philadelphia to Boston. It was the hottest day of the year and my cousin had on a woollen suit. By the time he reached Hartford, people in the car noticed that he had only two children with him. At Worcester he had only one. No one knew what had become of the others and no one asked. It seemed better not to ask. He reached Boston alone and never explained what had become of the tiny tots. Anyone who has ever travelled with tiny tots of his own, however, can guess.

The Social Life of the Newt

IT IS not generally known that the newt, although one of the smallest of our North American animals, has an extremely happy home-life. It is just one of those facts which never get bruited about.

I first became interested in the social phenomena of newt life early in the spring of 1913, shortly after I had finished my researches in sexual differentiation among amœba. Since that time I have practically lived among newts, jotting down observations, making lantern-slides, watching them in their work and in their play (and you may rest assured that the little rogues have their play—as who does not?) until, from much lying in a research posture on my stomach, over the enclosure in which they were confined, I found myself developing what I feared might be rudimentary creepers. And so, late this autumn, I stood erect and walked into my house, where I immediately set about the compilation of the notes I had made.

Since that time I have practically lived among the newts.

So much for the non-technical introduction. The remainder of this article bids fair to be fairly scientific.

In studying the more intimate phases of newt life, one is chiefly impressed with the methods by means of which the males force their attentions upon the females, with matrimony as an object. For the newt is, after all, only a newt, and has his weaknesses just as any of the rest of us. And I, for one, would not have it different. There is little enough fun in the world as it is.

The peculiar thing about a newt's courtship is its restraint. It is carried on, at all times, with a minimum distance of fifty paces (newt measure) between the male and the female. Some of the bolder males may now and then attempt to overstep the bounds of good sportsmanship and crowd in to forty-five paces, but such tactics are frowned upon by the Rules Committee. To the eye of an uninitiated observer, the pair might be dancing a few of the more open figures of the minuet.

The means employed by the males to draw the attention and win the affection of those of the opposite sex (females) are varied and extremely strategic. Until the valuable researches by Strudlehoff in 1887 (in his " *Entwickelungsmechanik* ") no one had been able to ascertain just what it was that the male newt did to make the female see anything in him worth throwing herself away on. It had been observed that the most personally unattractive newt could advance to within fifty paces of a female of his acquaintance and, by some *coup d'œil*, bring her to a point where she would, in no uncertain terms, indicate her willingness to go through with the marriage ceremony at an early date.

It was Strudlehoff who discovered, after watching several thousand courting newts under a magnifying lens (questionable taste on his part, without doubt, but all is fair in pathological love) that the male, during the courting season (the season opens on the tenth of March and extends through the following February, leaving about ten days for general overhauling and redecorating), gives forth a strange, phosphorescent glow from the centre of his highly coloured dorsal crest, somewhat similar in effect to the flash of a diamond scarf-pin in a red necktie. This glow, according to Strudlehoff, so fascinates the female with its air of elegance and indication of wealth, that she immediately falls a victim to its lure.

But the little creature, true to her sex-instinct, does not at once give evidence that her morale has been shattered. She affects a coyness and lack of interest, by hitching herself sideways along the bottom of the aquarium, with her head turned over her right shoulder away from the swain. A trained ear might even detect her whistling in an indifferent manner.

The male, in the meantime, is flashing his gleamer frantically two blocks away and is performing all sorts of attractive feats, calculated to bring the lady newt to terms. I have seen a male, in the stress of his handicap courtship, stand on his forefeet, gesticulating in amorous fashion with his hind feet in the air. Franz Ingehalt, in his " Über Weltschmerz des Newt," recounts having observed a distinct and deliberate undulation of the body, beginning with the shoulders and ending at the filament of the tail, which might well have been the origin of what is known to-day in scientific circles as " the shimmy." The object seems to be the same, except that in the case of the newt, it is the male who is the active agent.

In order to test the power of observation in the male during these manœuvres, I carefully removed the female, for whose benefit he was undulating, and put in her place, in slow succession, another (but less charming) female, a paper-weight of bronze shaped like a newt. and, finally, a common rubber eraser. From the distance at which the courtship was being carried on, the male (who was, it must be admitted, a bit near-sighted congenitally) was unable to detect the change in personnel, and continued, even in the presence of the rubber eraser, to gyrate and undulate in a most conscientious manner, still under the impression that he was making a conquest.

At last, worn out by his exertions, and disgusted at the meagreness of the reaction on the eraser, he gave a low cry of rage and despair and staggered to a nearby pan containing barley-water, from which he proceeded to drink himself into a gross stupor.

Thus, little creature, did your romance end, and who shall say that its ending was one whit less tragic than that of Camille? Not I, for one. . . . In fact, the two cases are not at all analogous.

And now that we have seen how wonderfully Nature works in the fulfilment of her laws, even among her tiniest creatures, let us study for a minute a cross-section of the community-life of the newt. It is a life full of all kinds of exciting adventure, from weaving nests to crawling about in the sun and catching insect larvæ and crustaceans. The newt's day is practically never done, largely because the insect larvæ multiply three million times as fast as the newt can possibly catch and eat them. And it takes the closest kind of community teamwork in the newt colony to get things anywhere near cleaned up by nightfall.

It is early morning, and the workers are just appearing hurrying to the old log which is to be the scene of their labours. What a scampering! What a bustle! Ah, little scamperers! Ah, little bustlers! How lucky you are, and how wise! You work long hours, without pay, for the sheer love of working. An ideal existence, I'll tell the scientific world.

Over here on the right of the log are the Master Draggers. Of all the newt workers, they are the most futile, which is high praise indeed. Come, let us look closer and see what it is that they are doing.

The one in the lead is dragging a bit of gurry out from the water and up over the edge into the sunlight. Following him, in single file, come the rest of the Master Draggers. They are not dragging anything, but are sort of helping the leader by crowding against him and eating little pieces out of the filament of his tail.

And now they have reached the top. The leader, by dint of much leg-work, has succeeded in dragging his prize to the ridge of the log.

The little workers, reaching the goal with their precious freight, are now giving it over to the Master Pushers, who have been waiting for them in the sun all this while. The Master Pushers' work is soon accomplished, for it consists simply in pushing the piece of gurry over the other side of the log until it falls with a splash into the water, where it is lost.

This part of their day's task finished, the tiny toilers rest, clustered together in a group, waving their heads about from side to side, as who should say: " There—that's done! " And so it *is* done, my little Master Draggers and my little Master Pushers, and *well* done, too. Would that my own work were as clean-cut and as satisfying.

And so it goes. Day in and day out, the busy army of newts go on making the world a better place in which to live. They have their little trials and tragedies, it is true, but they also have their fun, as any one can tell by looking at a logful of sleeping newts on a hot summer day.

And, after all, what more has life to offer?

The Lost
Language

AT the meeting of the International Philologists' Association in Lucerne in April (1923-1925), something in the nature of a bombshell was thrown by Professor Eric Nunsen of the University of Ulholm. Professor Nunsen, in a paper entitled, "Aryan Languages : The Funny Old Things," declared that in between the Hamitic group of languages and the Ural-Altaic group there should by rights come another and hitherto uncharted group, to be known as the Semi-Huinty group. Professor Nunsen's paper followed a number on the programme called " Al Holtz and His Six Musical Skaters."

According to this eminent philologist, too much attention has been paid in the past to root words. By " root words " we mean those words which look like roots of some kind or other when you draw pictures of them. These words recur in similar form in all the languages which comprise a certain group. Thus, in the Aryan group, compare, for example, the English *dish-towel*, Gothic *dersh-terl*, German *tish-döl*, Latin *dec-tola*, French *dis-toil*, Armenian *dash-taller*, Sanskrit *dit-tol* and Dutch *dösh-tooller*. In all of these words you will note the same absurdity.

In the same manner it is easy to trace the similarity between languages of the same group by noting, as in the Semitic group, that the fundamental *f* in Arabic becomes *w* in Assyrian, and the capital *G* in Phœnician becomes a small *g* in Abyssinian. This makes it hard for Assyrian travelling salesmen, as they have no place to leave their grips.

In his interesting work, " The Mutations of the Syllable *Bib* Between 2000 and 500 B.C.," Landoc Downs traces the use of the letter *h* down through Western Asia with the Caucasian migration into Central Europe, and there loses it. For perhaps two thousand years we have no record of the letter *h* being used by Nordics. This is perhaps not strange, as the Nordics at that time didn't use much of anything. And then suddenly, in about 1200 B.C., the letter *h* shows up again in Northern Ohio, this time under the alias of *m* and clean-shaven. There is no question, however, but that it is the old Bantu *h* in disguise, and we are thus able to tell that the two peoples (the Swiss and that other one) are really of the same basic stock. Anyone could tell that ; so don't be silly.

Now, says Professor Nunsen, it is quite probable that this change in root words, effected by the passage of the Aryan-speaking peoples north of the Danube, Dneiper and Don (the " D " in Danube is silent, making the word pronounced " Anube "), so irritated the Hamitic group (which included ancient Egyptian, Coptic, Berber and Otto H. Kahn) that they began dropping the final *g* just out of

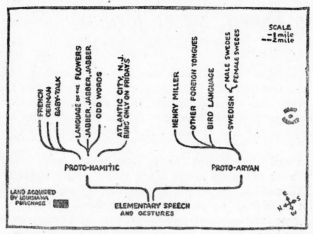

Chart showing relation of lost language (semi-Huinty) to the other Language groups and to itself.

spite. This, in the course of several centuries, resulted in the formation of a quite distinct group, the one which Professor Nunsen calls the " Semi-Huinty." It is not *entirely* Huinty, for there still remain traces of the old Hamitic. Just *semi*-Huinty. Even *semi* is quite a lot.

This, of course, takes no notice of the Ural-Altaic group. That is quite all right. No one ever does. This group includes the Lappish, Samoyed, Magyar and Tartar, and, as Dr. Kneeland Renfrew says in his " Useless Languages : Their Origin and Excuse " : " There is no sense in bothering with the Ural-Altaic group."

So Professor Nunsen has some authority for disregarding the question of grammatical gender, and it is on this point that he bases his discovery of the existence of the Semi-Huinty languages. These languages, he says, are monosyllabic and have no inflections, the tone used in uttering a word determining its meaning. In this it is similar to the Chinese tongue, which is one of the reasons why China is so far away from the European continent.

Thus the word *reezyl*, uttered in one tone, means " Here comes the postman," in another tone, " There is a button off this pair," and, in still a third tone, " you " (diminutive).

It will be seen from this how difficult it is for the philologist to do anything more than guess at just what the lost languages were really like. He is not sure that they are even lost. If they were *not* really lost, then the joke is on Professor Nunsen for having gone to all this trouble for nothing.

"Go Down, Sweet Jordan"

THERE used to be a time when four Negroes could get together and tear off a little ripe harmony and nobody thought anything of it except that it sounded great. Now, since spirituals have been taken up socially, you have got to know counterpoint and the " History of the Key of Four Flats " in order really to appreciate them.

What used to be just plain " Swing Low, Sweet Chariot " in the old brown book of college songs, along with " Seeing Nellie Home " and " Clementine," is now a manifestation of the growth of the Chariot Motif from the ancient African tap-dance through the muted eighth note into assonance and dissonance. And over your ears.

Having heard and read so much about the history of the Negro spiritual, I have been moved to look into the matter myself and have unearthed a large block of data which I am going to work into a book, to be called *The Legal Aspects of the Negro Spiritual*. It will take up the little known origins of the spiritual in Africa and bring it right down to the present day, or rather to December 5, when the book will come out (and go in again after seeing its own shadow).

Commentators and experts on the spiritual do not seem to realise that this particular form of harmony comes from the old African " vegetable-humming," dating back to the early seventeenth century and perhaps later. " Vegetable-humming " or *blakawa* was a chant taken part in by certain members of the tribe who wished they were vegetables and who thought that by humming loudly enough (with the tenor carrying the air) the God of the Harvest would turn them into vegetables and they could get their wish. There is no case on record of any one of them ever having been turned into a vegetable, but they kept on humming just the same, and it is in this strange form of religious ecstasy that the spiritual as we know it had its origin.

Let us take, for example, the spiritual, " Roll Down Jordan, Roll Up de Lord." This is one of the best songs for our purpose, as it contains the particular harmonic combinations which are also found in the " vegetable-humming," that is, C, G-sharp, A, and E, sliding up very wickedly into D-flat, G-natural, B-flat, and E-sharp. In case the G-sharp slips a little too much and gets into H, the singer must open his mouth very wide but stop making sounds altogether.

The first verse to " Roll Down Jordan, Roll Up de Lord " goes :

" Roll down Jordan ; roll up de Lord ;
  Roll down Jordan ; roll up de Lord ;
  Roll down Jordan ; roll up de Lord ;
  Roll down Jordan ; roll up de Lord ! "

We then find the whole spirit of the thing changing and the

evangelical note so common among Africans creeping into the second verse :

" Roll down de Lord ; roll up Jordan ;
    Roll down de Lord ; roll up Jordan ;
  Roll down de Lord ; roll up Jordan ;
    Roll down de Lord ; roll up Jordan ;
        Hey-hey ! "

Thus, you will see, does the modern chant derive from the old wheat-cake dance, which in its turn, derived from Chicago to Elkhart in four hours (baby talk). In this dance we seem to see the native women filing into the market-place in the early morning to offer up their prayer to the God of Corn on the Cob for better and more edible crops (" O God of the Harvest ! Give us some corn that we can eat. That last was terrible ! Amen "). The dance itself was taken part in by the local virgins and such young men of the tribe as were willing to be seen out with them. They marched once around the market-place beating drums until someone told them to shut up. Then they seated themselves in a semi-circle, facing inward, and rocked back and forth, back and forth. This made some of them sick and they had to be led out. The rest sat there rocking and crooning until they were eighteen years old, at which time they all got up and went home, pretty sore at themselves for having wasted so much time.

We have now seen how the old tribes handled the problem of what to sing and how to prevent people from singing it. The slave trade, bringing these Negroes and their descendants over to America, foisted the problem on the United States. For a long time, owing to the coloured people not knowing that they were developing a national folk song, nothing was done about it. The Negroes just sat around on piece of corn-pone and tried out various kinds of swipes which they aggravated by the use of the banjo. One of the favourite songs of this era ran thus :

(*Basses*)   M-m-m-m-m-m-m-m-m-m.
(*Tenors*)   M-m-m-m-m-m-m-m-m-m.
(*First tenor solo*)   M-m-m-m-m-m-m-m-m-m.
(*Second tenor solo*)   M-m-m-m-m-m-m-m-m-m.
(*Unison*)   Comin' fer to carry me home.

Under this ran the banjo accompaniment something like this :

Plunky-plunky-plunky-plunky,
Plunky-plunky-plunky-plunky,
Plunky-plunky-plunky-plunky,
Plunky-plunky-plunky-plunky,
Plunk !

Here we find for the first time some evidence of the spirit of the whole race stirring in its captivity. We seem to see the women filing into the market-place in the early morning to raise their prayer to the God of the Harvest—I guess that goes with the other song.

Gradually, during the Reconstruction Period following the Civil War, carpetbaggers from the North came in and organised these singing groups into glee-clubs, each with a leader and white gloves. They taught the basses to sing " Zum-zum-zum-zum " instead of " M-m-m-m-m-m-m " and wrote extra verses to many of the numbers to be sung as encores. The coloured people didn't know what to make of all this and many of them stopped singing entirely and went in for tap-dancing. But the popularisation of the Negro spiritual was on its way and special writers were assigned to the job of making up words which would sound rather native and yet would tell a story. It was found that only four words were needed for each song, as they were always repeated. Thus we have the growth of such songs as " Carryin' de Clouds on Jehovah's Back," " Ain't Gwine ter Pray fer de Old Black Roan," and " Ramona." The growth of the narrative in such songs can be traced in the following, entitled " All God's Fish is A-comin' Home " :

> " Oh, I went fer ter see de lightnin',
> Oh, I went fer ter see de lightnin',
> Oh, I went fer ter see de lightnin',
> But de lightnin' warn't ter home.

> " Oh, I went fer ter see de thunder,
> Oh, I went fer ter see de thunder,
> Oh, I went fer ter see de thunder,
> But de thunder warn't ter home.

> " Oh, I went fer ter see de rain (pronounced ' ray-un '),
> Oh, I went fer ter see de rain,
> Oh, I went fer ter see de rain,
> But de rain warn't ter home."

And so on the song goes, with the singer going to see, in rapid succession, the fog, the light mist, the snow, the oysters, the river, Lake Placid, the man about coming to carry away the ashes, and finally the Lord, none of them being at home except the Lord and he was busy.

This marks the final development of the spiritual as a regenerative force and also marks the point at which I give up. I would, however, like to hear four good coloured singers again without having to put my glasses on to follow the libretto.

Cleaning Out the Desk

THE first thing that I have got to do in my campaign to make this bright new year a better one for all of us is to clean out my desk. I started on this a little over a week ago, but so far, I have got only to the second drawer on the left hand side. I think that people must have been sneaking up during the last three or four years and putting things in my desk drawers while I have been asleep (they couldn't have done it while I was awake, for I have been working here every minute and would most certainly have noticed them at it, that is, unless they were dressed like gnomes. I never pay any attention to gnomes fussing around my desk when I am working. (In fact, I rather like it). But somebody has been at work, and hard at work, putting little objects and bits of paper in my desk drawers since the last time I went through them. And I don't know whether to throw them away or not.

For instance, what would I ever have wanted with an old mitten that I should have tucked it 'way back in that upper left hand drawer? It was right up against the back partition of the drawer, under a programme of the six-day bicycle race of February, 1933, and clinging to it, almost a part of it, was half a Life-Saver (clove flavour). Now, I never wear mittens, and even if I did it certainly wouldn't be a mitten like this. Furthermore, it has no mate. I haven't tried it on, for I would rather not have much to do with it in its present state, but I think it is for the right hand only. As I lift it gingerly out of the drawer (I was at first afraid that it was a small beaver) it seems to have some lumpy object tucked away up in the very tip, but I am not going in to find out what it is. I may have a man come up with a ferret and get the whole thing settled once and for all, but for the present both the mitten and the piece of Life-Saver are over in the corner of the room where I tossed them. I almost wish that they were back in the drawer again.

Just in front of the mitten, and a little to the left, I came upon a pile of old check book stubs (1936-38 inclusive, with February, April, July and August of 1936, and September to December of 1937 missing). On thumbing these over I was fascinated to see how many checks I had made out to " cash " and for what generous amounts. I must have been a pretty prodigal boy in those days. Dear me, dear me! Here is one made out to the Alsatian Novelty Company for $11.50 on Oct. 5, 1936. What traffic was I having with the Alsatian Novelty Company, do you suppose? Whatever it was, it wasn't enough of a novelty to make much impression on me— or on any one else, I guess. Maybe it was that rubber girdle that I sent for when I first began to notice that I was putting on weight. Whatever became of that, I wonder? I know what became of the weight, because it is right there where it was, but the girdle never did much but make me look bulky. Maybe the girdle is in the bottom drawer which I haven't come to yet.

Now about those old check stubs. I suppose that they might as well be thrown away, but then supposing the Alsatian Novelty Company should come around and say that I never paid the $11.50! I would be in a pretty pickle, wouldn't I? Of course, no jury would acquit me merely on the evidence of a check stub, but I don't know where the cancelled checks are and this would at least show that I was systematic about the thing. Then, too, the income tax people never get around to complaining about your payments until three or four years after they are made, and it might come in handy to be able to write them and say : " On March 15, 1938, according to my records, sent you a check for $45.60. It is up to you to find it." It might frighten them a little, anyway. So I guess the best thing to do is to put the stubs right back in the drawer and sit tight. All I hope is that no trouble arises over the checks drawn during those months which are lost. I wouldn't have a leg to stand on in that case.

In with the pile of check stubs I found a pamphlet entitled, " The Control of the Root Knot," issued by the U.S. Department of Agriculture in 1933. Now " root knot " is a thing that I never have had much trouble with (knock wood) and why I should have been saving a pamphlet on its control for seven years is something that not only mystifies, but irritates me a little. I read some of it and even then I didn't see why.

However, in 1933 I evidently thought that it might come in handy someday, and if I throw it away now it would be just my luck to come down with root knot next week and need it very badly. It is possible, of course, that I never had any hand in sending for the pamphlet at all and that it has been put in my desk by those mysterious agencies which I suspected at first (gnomes, or people representing themselves to be gnomes), in which case I am just making a fool of myself by hoarding it for another seven years. I guess that I will put it aside and read it thoroughly some day before throwing it away. Maybe my name is mentioned in it somewhere.

One article, however, which I recognised almost immediately is an old German pipe, one of those with a long, hooked stem and a bowl covered with straw. I think that I bought that myself; at any rate I remember trying to smoke it once or twice. But as soon as I got the tobacco into it and the fire started so that it would draw, it went out. This, I figured, was owing to my shutting the lid down over the bowl. The lid was evidently meant to be shut down, as there was a hinge on it (now fortunately broken so that it hangs loosely to one side), but I guess that I didn't quite have the knack of the thing, I remember thinking that sometime I might want to dress up in German costume for a lark or something, and then if I saved the pipe all I would have to get would be the German costume. So I saved it, and, as luck would have it, have never been called upon to dress up. There is still some of the original tobacco in it—some is in it and some is in the drawer—and I got a little sentimental over the memories of the old days in Munich where I bought it. (I was in Munich for three hours, between trains.) I even tried to smoke a little of it without clamping down the lid, but either the tobacco wasn't very good or my stomach isn't what it used to be, for I didn't go through with the scheme. "Wer nicht die Sehnsucht kennt—— " and whatever the rest of the quotation is.

   All of this, you will see, took up quite a lot of time. It is necessary that I get the desk cleaned out if I am ever going to start fresh now, but, with the first two drawers giving up such a wealth of sentimental memorabilia, I must evidently give over several days to it. There is, for instance, the letter from my insurance company, dated June 15, 1938, saying that as I have allowed policy No. 4756340 to lapse it will be necessary for me to take another physical examination before I can be reinstated. Now the question arises : Did I ever take the examination, and am I reinstated ? I remember taking an examination, but I think it was for the war. I certainly don't think that I have had my shirt off before a doctor since 1938 and I am afraid that if I call them up about it to find out they will make me do it right away, and that would be too bad because I wouldn't get anywhere near such a good mark now as I would have when the policy first lapsed. I might even have to do a lot of homework in order to catch up with my class. I think what I will do is set about right now getting into condition again and then call them up. I don't see how that letter ever got so far back in the drawer.
   There is one thing, however, that I shall never be short of again, and that is matches. I have never seen so many matches in one place as there were in my desk drawer. Here I have sat day after day, unable to work because I was out of matches with which to light my pipe, and all the time there were enough matches right under my nose (if I had put my nose in the upper left hand drawer) to do parlour tricks with for 10 years. They are all in those little paper covers, some containing five matches, some none, but, added together,

a magnificent hoard. I don't right now see the advantage of saving empty match covers, but I suppose I had some good reason at the time. Perhaps I liked the pictures on them. There are some with pictures of hotels on them which I have never visited in my life (Atlantic City has a marvellous representation) and I am afraid that I would have a difficult time denying that I had ever been to the Five Devils Inn in Tia Juana with such damning evidence as two match covers bearing its advertisement staring the examiners in the face. But honestly, I haven't. However, there are seven matches left in one and one match in the other; so I am going to save them anyway. And what a lot of fun I am going to have with my new-found treasure! It might even be the means of my becoming a pyromaniac.

But there! I mustn't think of such things now. All I have to do is get those other four drawers cleaned out and the papers which are on the back of my desk sorted out (I am a little nervous about tackling those papers, as I have heard a strange rustling in there lately and there might be field mice) and I shall be all spick and span and ready for the new year. All I hope is that the other drawers don't take as long as the first two have, or it will be 1941, and then I would have to wait until 1950 for another good, even year to start fresh.

Open Bookcases

THINGS have come to a pretty pass when a man can't buy a bookcase that hasn't got glass doors on it. What are we becoming—a nation of weaklings?

All over New York City I have been—trying to get something in which to keep books. And what am I shown? Curio cabinets, inclosed whatnots, museum cases in which to display fragments from the neolithic age, and glass-faced sarcophagi for dead butterflies.

" But I am apt to use my books at any time," I explain to the salesman. " I never can tell when it is coming on me. And when I want a book I want it quickly. I don't want to have to send down to the office for the key, and I don't want to have to manipulate any trick ball-bearings and open up a case as if I were getting cream-puffs out for a customer. I want a bookcase for books and not books for a bookcase."

(I really don't say all those clever things to the clerk. It took me quite a while to think them up. What I really say is, timidly, " Haven't you any bookcases without glass doors ? " and when they say " No," I thank them and walk into the nearest dining room table).

But if they keep on getting arrogant about it I shall speak up to them one of these fine days. When I ask for an open-faced bookcase they look with a scornful smile across the sales room toward the mahogany four-posters and say :

"Oh, no, we don't carry those any more. We don't have any call for them. Everyone uses the glass-doored ones now. They keep the books much cleaner."

Then the ideal procedure for a real book lover would be to keep his books in the original box, snugly packed in excelsior, with the lid nailed down. Then they would be nice and clean. And the sun couldn't get at them and ruin the bindings. Faugh! (Try saying that. It doesn't work out at all as you think it's going to. And it makes you feel very silly for having tried it).

Why, in the elder days bookcases with glass doors were owned only by people who filled them with ten volumes of a pictorial history of the Civil War (including some swell steel engravings), "Walks and Talks with John L. Stoddard" and "Daily Thoughts for Daily Needs," done in robin's egg blue with a watered silk bookmark dangling out. A set of Sir Walter Scott always helps fill out a bookcase with glass doors. It looks well from the front and shows that you know good literature when you see it. And you don't have to keep opening and shutting the doors to get it out, for you never want to get it out.

A bookcase with glass doors used to be a sign that somewhere in the room there was a crayon portrait of Father when he was a young man, with a real piece of glass stuck on the portrait to represent a diamond stud.

And now we are told that "everyone buys bookcases with glass doors; we have no call for others." Soon we shall be told that the thing to do is to buy the false backs of bindings, such as they have in stage libraries, to string across behind the glass. It will keep us from reading too much, and then, too, no one will want to borrow our books.

But one clerk told me the truth. And I am just fearless enough to tell it here. I know that it will kill my chances for the Presidency, but I cannot stop to think of that.

After advising me to have a carpenter build me the kind of bookcase I wanted, and after I had told him that I had my name in for a carpenter but wasn't due to get him until late in the fall, as he was waiting for prices to go higher before taking the job on, the clerk said :

" That's it. It's the price. You see the furniture manufacturers can make much more money out of a bookcase with glass doors than they can without. When by hanging glass doors on a piece of furniture at but little more expense to themselves they can get a much bigger profit, what's the sense in making them without glass doors? They have just stopped making them, that's all."

So you see the American people are being practically forced into buying glass doors whether they want them or not. Is that right? Is it fair? Where is our personal liberty going to? What is becoming of our traditional American institutions?

I don't know.

"Coffee, Megg and Ilk, Please"

GIVE me any topic in current sociology, such as " The Working Classes *vs.* the Working Classes," or " Various Aspects of the Minimum Wage," and I can talk on it with considerable confidence. I have no hesitation in putting the Workingman, as such, in his place among the hewers of wood and drawers of water—a necessary adjunct to our modern life, if you will, but of little real consequence in the big events of the world.

But when I am confronted, in the flesh, by the " close up " of a workingman with any vestige of authority, however small, I immediately lose my perspective—and also my poise. I become servile, almost cringing. I feel that my modest demands on his time may, uness tactfully presented, be offensive to him and result in something, lI haven't been able to analyse just what, perhaps public humiliation.

For instance, whenever I enter an elevator in a public building I am usually repeating to myself the number of the floor at which I wish to alight. The elevator man gives the impression of being a social worker, filling the job just for that day to help out the regular elevator man, and I feel that the least I can do is to show him that I know what's what. So I don't tell him my floor number as soon as I get in. Only elderly ladies do that. I keep whispering it over to myself, thinking to tell it to the world when the proper time comes. But then the big question arises—what is the proper time ?

If I want to get out at the eighteenth floor, should I tell him at the sixteenth or the seventeenth ? I decide on the sixteenth and frame my lips to say, " Eighteen out, please." (Just why one should have to add the word " out " to the number of the floor is not clear. When you say " eighteen " the obvious construction of the phrase is that you want to get *out* at the eighteenth floor, not that you want to get *in* there or be let down through the flooring of the car at that point. However, you'll find the most sophisticated elevator riders, namely, messenger boys, always adding the word " out," and it is well to follow what the messenger boys do in such matters if you don't want to go wrong.)

So there I am, mouthing the phrase, " Eighteen out, please," as we shoot past the tenth—eleventh—twelfth—thirteenth floors. Then I begin to get panicky. Supposing that I should forget my lines ! Or that I should say them too soon ! Or too late ! We are now at the fifteenth floor. I clear my throat. Sixteen ! Hoarsely I murmur, " Eighteen out." But at the same instant a man with a cigar in his mouth bawls, " Seventeen out ! " and I am not heard. The car stops at seventeen, and I step confidentially up to the elevator man and repeat, with an attempt at nonchalance, " Eighteen out, please." But just as I say the words the door clangs, drowning out my request, and we shoot up again. I make another attempt, but have become inarticulate and succeed only in making a noise like a man strangling. And by this time we are at the twenty-first floor with no relief in sight. Shattered, I retire to the back of the car and ride up to the roof and down again, trying to look as if I worked in the building and had to do it, however boresome it might be. On the return trip I don't care what the elevator man thinks of me, and tell him at every floor that I, personally, am going to get off at the eighteenth, no matter what any one else in the car does. I am dictatorial enough when I am riled. It is only in the opening rounds that I hug the ropes.

My timidity when dealing with minor officials strikes me first in my voice. I have any number of witnesses who will sign statements to the effect that my voice changed about twelve years ago, and that in ordinary conversation my tone, if not especially virile, is at least consistent and even. But when, for instance, I give an order at a soda fountain, if the clerk overawes me at all, my voice breaks into a yodel that makes the phrase " Coffee, egg and milk " a pretty snatch of song, but practically worthless as an order.

If the soda counter is lined with customers and the clerks so busy tearing up checks and dropping them into the toy banks that they seem to resent any call on their drink-mixing abilities, I might just as well save time and go home and shake up an egg and milk for myself, for I shall not be waited on until every one else has left the counter and they are putting the nets over the caramels for the night. I know that. I've gone through it too many times to be deceived.

For there is something about the realisation that I must shout out my order ahead of some one else that absolutely inhibits my shouting powers. I will stand against the counter, fingering my ten-cent check and waiting for the clerk to come near enough for me to tell him what I want, while, in the meantime, ten or a dozen people have edged up next to me and given their orders, received their

At the same instant a man with a cigar in his mouth bawls, " Seventeen out ! "

drinks and gone away. Every once in a while I catch a clerk's eye and lean forward murmuring, " Coffee "—but that is as far as I get. Some one else has shoved his way in and shouted, " Coca-Cola," and I draw back to get out of the way of the vichy spray. (Incidentally, the men who push their way in and footfault on their orders always ask for " Coca-Cola." Somehow it seems like painting the lily for them to order a nerve tonic.)

I then decide that the thing for me to do is to speak up loud and act brazenly. So I clear my throat, and, placing both hands on the counter, emit what promises to be a perfect bellow: " COFFEE, MEGG AND ILK." This makes just about the impression you'd think it would, both on my neighbours and the clerk, especially as it is delivered in a tone which ranges from a rich baritone to a rather rasping tenor. At this I withdraw and go to the other end of the counter, where I can begin life over again with a clean slate.

Here, perhaps, I am suddenly confronted by an impatient clerk who is in a perfect frenzy to grab my check and tear it into bits to drop in his box. " What's yours ? " he flings at me. I immediately lose my memory and forget what it was that I wanted. But here is a man who has a lot of people to wait on and who doubtless gets paid according to the volume of business he brings in. I have no right to interfere with his work. There is a big man edging his way beside me who is undoubtedly going to shout " Coca-Cola " in half a second. So I beat him to it and say, " Coca-Cola," which is probably the last drink in the store that I want to buy. But it is the only thing that I can remember at the moment, in spite of the fact that I have been thinking all morning how a coffee, egg and milk would taste. I suppose that one of the psychological principles of advertising is to so hammer the name of your product into the mind of the timid buyer that when he is confronted by a brusque demand for an order he can't think of anything else to say, whether he wants it or not.

This dread of offending the minor official or appearing at a disadvantage before a clerk extends even to my taking nourishment. I don't think that I have ever yet gone into a restaurant and ordered exactly what I wanted. If only the waiter would give me the card and let me alone for, say, fifteen minutes, as he does when I want to get him to bring me my check, I could work out a meal along the lines of what I like. But when he stands over me, with disgust clearly registered on his face, I order the thing I like least and consider myself lucky to get out of it with so little disgrace.

And yet I have no doubt that if one could see him in his family life the Workingman is just an ordinary person like the rest of us. He is probably not at all as we think of him in our dealings with him— a harsh, dictatorial, intolerant autocrat, but rather a kindly soul who likes nothing better than to sit by the fire with his children and read.

And he would probably be the first person to scoff at the idea that he could frighten me.

A Good Old-Fashioned Christmas

SOONER or later at every Christmas party, just as things are beginning to get good, someone shuts his eyes, puts his head back and moans softly : " Ah, well, this isn't like the old days. We don't seem to have any good old-fashioned Christmases any more." To which the answer from my corner of the room is : " All right! That suits me ! "

Just what they have in mind when they say " old-fashioned Christmas " you never can pin them down to telling. " Lots of snow," they mutter, " and lots of food." Yet, if you work it right, you can still get plenty of snow and food to-day. Snow, at any rate.

Then there seems to be some idea of the old-fashioned Christmas being, of necessity, in the country. It doesn't make any difference whether you were raised on a farm or whether your ideas of a rural Christmas were gleaned from pictures in old copies of " Harper's Young People," you must give folks to understand that such were the surroundings in which you spent your childhood holidays. And that, ah, me, those days will never come again !

Well, supposing you get your wish some time. Supposing, let us say, your wife's folks who live up in East Russet, Vermont, write and ask you to come up and bring the children for a good old-fashioned Christmas, " while we are all still together," they add cheerily with their flair for putting everybody in good humour.

Hurray, hurray ! Off to the country for Christmas ! Pack up all the warm clothes in the house, for you will need them up there where the air is clean and cold. Snow-shoes ? Yes, put them in, or better yet, Daddy will carry them. What fun ! Take along some sleigh-bells to jangle in case there aren't enough on the pung. There must be jangling sleigh-bells. And whisky for frost-bite. Or is it snake-bite that whisky is for ? Anyway, put it in ! We're off ! Good-bye, all ! Good-bye ! JANGLE-JANGLE-JANGLE-Jangle-Jangle-Jangle-jangle-jangle-jangle-jangle-jangle-jangle !

In order to get to East Russet you take the Vermont Central as far as Twitchell's Falls and change there for Torpid River Junction, where a spur line takes you right into Gormley. At Gormley you are met by a buckboard which takes you back to Torpid River Junction again. By this time a train or something has come in which will wait for the local from Besus. While waiting for this you will have time to send your little boy to school, so that he can finish the third grade.

At East Russet Grandpa meets you with the sleigh. The bags are piled in and Mother sits in front with Lester in her lap while Daddy takes Junior and Ga-Ga in back with him and the luggage. Giddap, Esther Girl !

Esther Girl giddaps, and two suitcases fall out. Heigh-ho ! Out we get and pick them up, brushing the snow off and filling our cuffs

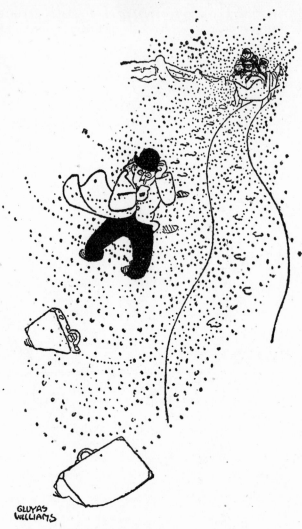

Esther Girl giddaps, and two suitcases fall out.

with it as we do so. After all, there is nothing like snow for getting up one's cuffs. Good clean snow never hurt anyone. Which is lucky, because after you have gone a mile or so, you discover that Ga-Ga is missing. Never mind, she is a self-reliant little girl and will doubtless find her way to the farm by herself. Probably she will be there waiting for you when you arrive.

The farm is situated on a hill about eleven hundred miles from the centre of town, just before you get into Canada. If there is a breeze in winter, they get it. But what do they care for breezes, so long as they have the Little Colonel oil-heater in the front room, to make everything cosy and warm within a radius of four inches! And the big open fireplace with the draught coming down it! Fun for everybody!

You are just driving up to the farmhouse in the sleigh, with the entire right leg frozen where the lap robe has slipped out. Grandma is waiting for you at the door and you bustle in, all glowing with good cheer. "Merry Christmas, Grandma!" Lester is cross and Junior is asleep and has to be dragged by the hand upstairs, bumping against each step all the way. It is so late that you decide that you all might as well go to bed, especially as you learn that breakfast is at four-thirty. It usually is at four, but Christmas being a holiday everyone sleeps late.

As you reach the top of the stairs you get into a current of cold air which has something of the quality of the temperature in a nice well-regulated crypt. This is the Bedroom Zone, and in it the thermometer never tops the zero mark from October fifteenth until the middle of May. Those rooms in which no one sleeps are used to store perishable vegetables in, and someone has to keep thumbing the tomatoes and pears every so often to prevent their getting so hard that they crack.

The way to get undressed for bed in one of Grandpa's bedrooms is as follows: Starting from the foot of the stairs where it is warm, run up two at a time to keep the circulation going as long as possible. Opening the bedroom door with one hand, tear down the curtains from the windows with the other, pick up the rugs from the floor and snatch the spread from the top of the bureau. Pile all these on the bed, cover with the closet door which you have wrenched from its hinges, and leap quickly underneath. It sometimes helps to put on a pair of rubbers over your shoes.

And even when you are in bed, you have no guarantee of going to sleep. Grandpa's mattresses seem to contain the overflow from the silo, corn-husks, baked potato skins and long, stringy affairs which feel like pipe cleaners. On a cold night, snuggling down into these is about like snuggling down into a bed of damp pine cones out in the forest.

Then there are Things abroad in the house. Shortly after you get into bed, the stairs start snapping. Next something runs along the roof over your head. You say to yourself: "Don't be silly. It's only Santa Claus." Then it runs along in the wall behind the head of the bed. Santa Claus wouldn't do that. Down the long hall which leads into the ell of the house you can hear the wind sighing softly, with an occasional reassuring bang of a door.

The unmistakable sound of someone dying in great pain rises from just below the window sill. It is a sort of low moan, with just a touch of strangulation in it. Perhaps Santa has fallen off the roof. Perhaps that story you once heard about Grandpa's house having been a hang-out for revolutionary smugglers is true, and one of the smugglers has come back for his umbrella. The only place at a time like this is down under the bedclothes. But the children

C

become frightened and demand to be taken home, and Grandpa has to be called to explain that it is only Blue Bell out in the barn. Blue Bell has asthma, and on a cold night they have to be very patient with her.

Christmas morning dawns cloudy and cold, with the threat of plenty more snow, and, after all, what would Christmas be without snow? You lie in bed for one hour and a quarter trying to figure out how you can get up without losing the covers from around you. A glance at the water pitcher shows that it is time for them to put the red ball up for skating. You think of the nice warm bathroom at home, and decide that you can wait until you get back there before shaving.

This breaking the ice in the pitcher seems to be a feature of the early lives of all great men which they look back on with tremendous satisfaction. " When I was a boy, I used to have to break the ice in the pitcher every morning before I could wash," is said with as much pride as one might say, " When I was a boy I stood at the head of my class." Just what virtue there is in having to break ice in a pitcher is not evident, unless it lies in their taking the bother to break the ice and wash at all. Anytime that I have to break ice in a pitcher as a preliminary to washing, I go unwashed, that's all. And Benjamin Franklin and U. S. Grant and Rutherford B. Hayes can laugh as much as they like. I'm nobody's fool about a thing like that.

Getting the children dressed is a lot of fun when you have to keep

The entire family enters, purple and chattering and exceedingly cross.

pumping their limbs up and down to keep them from freezing out stiff. The children love it and are just as bright and merry as little pixies when it is time to go downstairs and say " Good morning " to Grandpa and Grandma. The entire family enters the dining room purple and chattering and exceedingly cross.

After breakfast everyone begins getting dinner. The kitchen being the only warm place in the house may have something to do with it. But before long there are so many potato peelings and turkey feathers and squash seeds and floating bits of pie crust in the kitchen that the women folk send you and the children off into the front part of the house to amuse yourselves and get out of the way.

Then what a jolly time you and the kiddies and Grandpa have together ! You can either slide on the horse hair sofa, or play " The Wayside Chapel " on the piano (the piano has scroll work on either side of the music rack with yellow silk showing through), or look out the window and see ten miles of dark grey snow. Perhaps you may even go out to the barn and look at the horses and cows, but really, as you walk down between the stalls, when you have seen one horse or one cow you have seen them all. And besides, the cold in the barn has an added flavour of damp harness leather and musty carriage upholstery which eats into your very marrow.

Of course, there are the presents to be distributed, but that takes on much the same aspect as the same ceremony in the new-fashioned Christmas, except that in the really old-fashioned Christmas the presents weren't so tricky. Children got mostly mittens and shoes, with a sled thrown in sometimes for dissipation. Where a boy to-day is bored by three o'clock in the afternoon with his electric grain elevator and miniature pond with real perch in it, the old-fashioned boy was lucky if he got a copy of " Naval Battles of the War of 1812 " and an orange. Now this feature is often brought up in praise of the old way of doing things. " I tell you," says Uncle Gyp, " the children in my time never got such presents as you get to-day." And he seems proud of the fact, as if there were some virtue accruing to him for it. If the children of to-day can get electric grain elevators and tin automobiles for Christmas, why aren't they that much better off than their grandfathers who got only wristlets ? Learning the value of money, which seems to be the only argument of the stand-patters, doesn't hold very much water as a Christmas slogan. The value of money can be learned in just about five minutes when the time comes, but Christmas is not the season.

But to return to the farm, where you and the kiddies and Gramp' are killing time. You can either bring in wood from the wood shed, or thaw out the pump, or read the books in the bookcase over the writing desk. Of the three, bringing in the wood will probably be the most fun, as you are likely to burn yourself thawing out the pump, and the list of reading matter on hand includes " The Life and Deeds of General Grant," " Our First Century," " Andy's Trip to Portland," bound volumes of the Jersey Cattle Breeders' Gazette and " Diseases of the Horse." Then there are some old copies of " Round the Lamp" for the years 1850-54 and some coloured plates showing plans for the approaching World's Fair at Chicago.

Thus the time passes, in one round of gaiety after another, until you are summoned to dinner. Here all caviling must cease. The dinner lives up to the advertising. If an old-fashioned Christmas could consist entirely of dinner without the old-fashioned bedrooms, the old-fashioned pitcher, and the old-fashioned entertainments, we professional pessimists wouldn't have a turkey leg to stand on. But, as has been pointed out, it is possible to get a good dinner without going up to East Russet, Vt., or, if it isn't, then our civilisation has been a failure.

And the dinner only makes the aftermath seem worse. According to an old custom of the human race, everyone over eats. Deliberately and with considerable gusto you sit at the table and say pleasantly: "My, but I won't be able to walk after this. Just a little more of the dark meat, please, Grandpa, and just a dab of stuffing. Oh, dear, that's too much!" You haven't the excuse of the drunkard, who becomes oblivious to his excesses after several drinks. You know what you are doing, and yet you make light of it and even laugh about it as long as you *can* laugh without splitting out a seam.

Then you sit and moan.

And then you sit and moan. If you were having a good new-fashioned Christmas you could go out to the movies or take a walk, or a ride, but to be really old-fashioned you must stick close to the house, for in the old days there were no movies and no automobiles and if you wanted to take a walk you had to have the hired man go ahead of you with a snow-shovel and make a tunnel. There are probably plenty of things to do in the country to-day, and just as many automobiles and electric lights as there are in the city, but you can't call Christmas with all these improvements " an old-fashioned Christmas." That's cheating.

If you are going through with the thing right, you have got to retire to the sitting room after dinner and *sit*. Of course, you can go out and play in the snow if you want to, but you know as well as I do that this playing in the snow is all right when you are small but a bit trying on anyone over thirty. And anyway, it always began to snow along about three in the afternoon an old-fashioned Christmas day, with a cheery old leaden sky overhead and a jolly old gale sweeping around the corners of the house.

No, you simply must sit indoors, in front of a fire if you insist, but nevertheless with nothing much to do. The children are sleepy and snarling. Grandpa is just sleepy. Someone tries to start the conversation, but everyone else is too gorged with food to be able to move the lower jaw sufficiently to articulate. It develops that the family is in possession of the loudest ticking clock in the world and along about four o'clock it begins to break its own record. A stenographic report of the proceedings would read as follows :

" Ho-hum ! I'm sleepy ! I shouldn't have eaten so much."

" Tick-tock-tick-tock-tick-tock-tick-tock— "

" It seems just like Sunday, doesn't it ? "

" Look at Grandpa ! He's asleep."

" Here, Junior ! Don't plague Grandpa. Let him sleep."

" Tick-tock-tick-tock-tick-tock— "

" Junior ! Let Grandpa alone ! Do you want Mamma to take you upstairs ? "

" Ho-hum ! "

" Tick-tock-tick-tock-tick-tock— "

Louder and louder the clock ticks, until something snaps in your brain and you give a sudden leap into the air with a scream, finally descending to strangle each of the family in turn, and Grandpa as he sleeps. Then, as you feel your end is near, all the warm things you have ever known come back to you, in a flash. You remember the hot Sunday subway to Coney, your trip to Mexico, the bullfighters of Spain.

You dash out into the snowdrifts and plunge along until you sink exhausted. Only the fact that this article ends here keeps you from freezing to death, with an obituary the next day reading :

" DIED suddenly, at East Russet, Vt., of an old-fashioned Christmas."

The Benchley-Whittier
Correspondence

OLD scandals concerning the private life of Lord Byron have been revived with the recent publication of a collection of his letters. One of the big questions seems to be : *Did Byron send Mary Shelley's letter to Mrs. R. B. Hoppner?* Everyone seems greatly excited about it.

Lest future generations be thrown into turmoil over my correspondence after I am gone, I want right now to clear up the mystery which has puzzled literary circles for over thirty years. I need hardly add that I refer to what is known as the " Benchley-Whittier Correspondence."

The big question over which both my biographers and Whittier's might possibly come to blows is this, as I understand it : *Did John Greenleaf Whittier ever receive the letters I wrote to him in the late Fall of* 1890? *If he did not, who did? And under what circumstances were they written?*

I was a very young man at the time, and Mr. Whittier was, naturally, very old. There had been a meeting of the Save-Our-Song-Birds Club in old Dane Hall (now demolished) in Cambridge, Massachusetts. Members had left their coats and hats in the check-room at the foot of the stairs (now demolished).

In passing out after a rather spirited meeting, during the course of which Mr. Whittier and Dr. Van Blarcom had opposed each other rather violently over the question of Baltimore orioles, the aged poet naturally was the first to be helped into his coat. In the general mix-up (there was considerable good-natured fooling among the members as they left, relieved as they were from the strain of the meeting) Whittier was given my hat by mistake. When I came to go, there was nothing left for me but a rather seedy grey derby with a black band, containing the initials " J. G. W." As the poet was visiting in Cambridge at the time I took opportunity next day to write the following letter to him :

Cambridge, Mass.
November 7, 1890.

Dear Mr. Whittier :

I am afraid that in the confusion following the Save-Our-Song-Birds meeting last night, you were given my hat by mistake. I have yours and will gladly exchange it if you will let me know when I may call on you.

May I not add that I am a great admirer of your verse ? Have you ever tried any musical comedy lyrics ? I think that I could get you in on the ground floor in the show game, as I know a young man who has written several songs which E. E. Rice has said he would like to use in his next comic opera—provided he can get words to go with them.

But we can discuss all this at our meeting, which I hope will be soon, as your hat looks like hell on me.

Yours respectfully,
ROBERT C. BENCHLEY.

I am quite sure that this letter was mailed, as I find an entry in my diary of that date which reads :

" Mailed a letter to J. G. Whittier.   Cloudy and cooler."

Furthermore, in a death-bed confession, some ten years later, one Mary F. Rourke, a servant employed in the house of Dr. Agassiz, with whom Whittier was bunking at the time, admitted that she herself had taken a letter, bearing my name in the corner of the envelope, to the poet at his breakfast on the following morning.

But whatever became of it after it fell into his hands, I received no reply.   I waited five days, during which time I stayed in the house rather than go out wearing the Whittier grey derby.   On the sixth day I wrote him again, as follows :

Cambridge, Mass.
Nov. 14, 1890.

Dear Mr. Whittier :
How about that hat of mine ?

Yours respectfully,
ROBERT C. BENCHLEY.

I received no answer to this letter either.   Concluding that the good grey poet was either too busy or too gosh-darned mean to bother with the thing, I myself adopted an attitude of supercilious unconcern and closed the correspondence with the following terse message :

Cambridge, Mass.
December 4, 1890.

Dear Mr. Whittier :
It is my earnest wish that the hat of mine which you are keeping will slip down over your eyes some day, interfering with your vision to such an extent that you will walk off the sidewalk into the gutter and receive painful, albeit superficial, injuries.

Your young friend,
ROBERT C. BENCHLEY.

Here the matter ended so far as I was concerned, and I trust that biographers in the future will not let any confusion of motives or misunderstanding of dates enter into a clear and unbiassed statement of the whole affair.   We must not have another Shelley-Byron scandal.

The Romance of Digestion

WHEN you take a bite of that delicious cookie, or swallow a morsel of that nourishing bread, do you stop to think of the marvellous and intricate process by means of which Mother Nature is going to convert it into bone and sinew and roses for those pretty cheeks? Probably not, and it is just as well. For if you did stop to think of it at that time, you would unquestionably not be able to digest that cookie—or that nourishing bread.

But whether you think of it or not this exciting process of digestion is going on, day in and day out, sometimes pretty badly but always with a great show of efficiency. It is, on the whole, probably one of the worst-done jobs in the world.

First you must know that those hard, white edges of bone which you must have noticed hundreds of times along the front of your mouth, are "teeth," and are put there for a very definite purpose. They are the ivory gates to the body. They are Nature's tiny sentinels, and if you have ever bitten yourself, you will know how sharp they can be, and what efficient little watchmen they are. Just you try to slip your finger into your mouth without your teeths' permission, and see how far you get. Or try to get it out, once they have captured it.

Now these thousands of brave little soldiers, the teeth, which we have in our mouths, take the food as it comes through the air (in case you are snapping at a butterfly) or from the fork, and separate it into its component parts (air, land and water). In this process, the teeth are aided by the tongue, which is that awful looking thing right back of your teeth. Don't look at it!

The tongue (which we may call the escalator of the mouth or Nature's nobleman for short), and the teeth toss the food back and forth between them until there is nothing left of it, except the little bones which you have to take out between your thumb and forefinger and lay on your butter-plate. In doing this be careful that the bone is really on the butter-plate and that it does not stick to your finger so that you put it back into your mouth again on the next trip, for this would make the little white sentries very angry and they might all drop out.

And now comes the really wonderful part of the romance which is being enacted right there under your very eyes. A chemical reaction on the tongue presses a little button which telegraphs down, down, down, 'way down to the cross old Stomach and says: "Please, sir, do you want this food or don't you?" And the Stomach, whom we shall call "Prince Charming" from now on, telegraphs (or more likely writes) back: "Yes, dear!" or "You can do what you like with it for all of me." Just as he happens to feel at the time.

And then, such a hurry and bustle as goes on in the mouth! "Foodie's going to visit Stomach!" all the little teeth cry, and rush

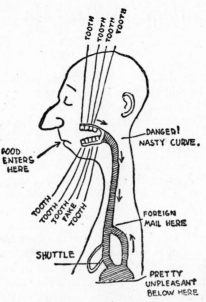

Cross section of human food duct, showing ludicrous
process of self-styled " Digestion."

about for all the world as if they were going themselves. " All aboard, all aboard ! " calls out the tongue, and there is a great ringing of bells and blowing of whistles and bumping of porters and in the midst of it all, the remnants of that delicious cookie seated nervously on the tongue, ready to be taken down on its first journey alone, down to see Prince Charming. For all the joyousness of the occasion, it is a little sad, too. For that bit of cookie is going to get some terribly tough treatment before it is through.

The food is then placed on a conveyor, by means of which it is taken to the Drying Room, situated on the third floor, where it is taken apart and washed and dried, preparatory to going through the pressing machines. These pressing machines are operated by one man, who stands by the conveyor as it brings the food along and tosses it into the vats. Here all rocks and moss are drawn off by mechanical pickers and the food subjected to treatment in a solution of sulphite, a secret process which is jealously guarded. From here the food is taken to the Playroom where it plays around awhile with the other children until it is time for it to be folded by the girls in the bindery, packed into neat stacks, and wrapped for shipment in bundles of fifty. Some of these bundles, the proteins, are shipped to the bones of the body, others, the hydrates, go to making muscle, while a third class, the sophomores, contribute to making fatty tissue which nobody wants, that is, not if he has any pride at all about his appearance. The by-products are made into milk bottle caps, emery wheels, and insurance calendars, and are sold at cost.

Thus we see how wonderfully Nature takes care of us and our little troubles, aided only by soda-mint and bicarbonate.

What College Did to Me

An Outline of Education

MY college education was no haphazard affair. My courses were all selected with a very definite aim in view, with a serious purpose in mind—no classes before eleven in the morning or after two-thirty in the afternoon, and nothing on Saturday at all. That was my slogan. On that rock was my education built.

As what is known as the Classical Course involved practically no afternoon laboratory work, whereas in the Scientific Course a man's time was never his own until 4 p.m. anyway, I went in for the classic. But only such classics as allowed for a good sleep in the morning. A man has his health to think of. There is such a thing as being a studying fool.

In my days (I was a classmate of the founder of the college) a student could elect to take any courses in the catalogue, provided no two of his choices came at the same hour. The only things he was not supposed to mix were Scotch and gin. This was known as the Elective System. Now I understand that the boys have to have, during the four years, at least three courses beginning with the same letter. This probably makes it very awkward for those who like to get away of a Friday afternoon for the week-end.

Under the Elective System my schedule was somewhat as follows :

Mondays, Wednesdays and Fridays at 11.00 :
   Botany 2a (The History of Flowers and Their Meaning)
Tuesdays and Thursdays at 11.00 :
   English 26 (The Social Life of the Minor Sixteenth Century Poets)
Mondays, Wednesdays and Fridays at 12.00 :
   Music 9 (History and Appreciation of the Clavichord)
Tuesdays and Thursdays at 12.00 :
   German 12b (Early Minnesingers—Walter von Vogelweider, Ulric Glannsdorf and Freimann von Stremhofen. Their Songs and Times)
Mondays, Wednesdays and Fridays at 1.30 :
   Fine Arts 6 (Doric Columns : Their Uses, History and Various Heights)
Tuesdays and Thursdays at 1.30 :
   French 1c (Exceptions to the verb *être*)

This was, of course, just one year's work. The next year I followed these courses up with supplementary courses in the history of lace making, Russian taxation systems before Catharine the Great, North American glacial deposits and Early Renaissance etchers.

This gave me a general idea of the progress of civilisation and a certain practical knowledge which has stood me in good stead in thousands of ways since my graduation.

My system of studying was no less strict. In lecture courses I had my notebooks so arranged that one-half of the page could be devoted to drawings of five-pointed stars (exquisitely shaded), girls' heads, and tick-tack-toe. Some of the drawings in my economics notebook in the course on Early English Trade Winds were the

*Some of the drawings in my economic notebook were the finest things
I have ever done.*

finest things I have ever done. One of them was a whole tree (an oak) with every leaf in perfect detail. Several instructors commented on my work in this field.

These notes I would take home after the lecture, together with whatever supplementary reading the course called for. Notes and textbooks would then be placed on a table under a strong lamplight. Next came the sharpening of pencils, which would take perhaps fifteen minutes. I had some of the best sharpened pencils in college. These I placed on the table beside the notes and books.

At this point it was necessary to light a pipe, which involved going to the table where the tobacco was. As it so happened, on the same table was a poker hand, all dealt, lying in front of a vacant chair. Four other chairs were oddly enough occupied by students, also preparing to study. It therefore resolved itself into something of a seminar, or group conference, on the courses under discussion. For example, the first student would say :

" I can't open."

The second student would perhaps say the same thing.

The third student would say : " I'll open for fifty cents."

And the seminar would be on.

At the end of the seminar, I would go back to my desk, pile the notes and books on top of each other, put the light out, and go to bed, tired but happy in the realisation that I had not only spent the evening busily but had helped put four of my friends through college.

An inventory of stock acquired at college discloses the following bits of culture and erudition which have nestled in my mind after all these years.

THINGS I LEARNED FRESHMAN YEAR

1. Charlemagne either died or was born or did something with the Holy Roman Empire in 800.

2. By placing one paper bag inside another paper bag you can carry home a milk shake in it.

3. There is a double l in the middle of " parallel."

4. Powder rubbed on the chin will take the place of a shave if the room isn't very light.

5. French nouns ending in " aison " are feminine.

6. Almost everything you need to know about a subject is in the encyclopedia.

7. A tasty sandwich can be made by spreading peanut butter on raisin bread.

8. A floating body displaces its own weight in the liquid in which it floats.

9. A sock with a hole in the toe can be worn inside out with comparative comfort.

10. The chances are against filling an inside straight.

11. There is a law in economics called *The Law of Diminishing Returns*, which means that after a certain margin is reached returns begin to diminish. This may not be correctly stated, but there *is* a law by that name.

12. You begin tuning a mandolin with A and tune the other strings from that.

SOPHOMORE YEAR

1. A good imitation of measles rash can be effected by stabbing the forearm with a stiff whisk-broom.

2. Queen Elizabeth was not above suspicion.

3. In Spanish you pronounce z like th.

4. Nine-tenths of the girls in a girls' college are not pretty.

5. You can sleep undetected in a lecture course by resting the head on the hand as if shading the eyes.

6. Weakness in drawing technique can be hidden by using a wash instead of black and white line.

7. Quite a respectable bun can be acquired by smoking three or

four pipefuls of strong tobacco when you have no food in your stomach.

8. The ancient Phœnicians were really Jews, and got as far north as England where they operated tin mines.

9. You can get dressed much quicker in the morning if the night before when you are going to bed you take off your trousers and underdrawers at once, leaving the latter inside the former.

JUNIOR YEAR

1. Emerson left his pastorate because he had some argument about communion.

2. All women are untrustworthy.

3. Pushing your arms back as far as they will go fifty times each day increases your chest measurement.

4. Marcus Aurelius had a son who turned out to be a bad boy.

5. Eight hours of sleep are not necessary.

6. Heraclitus believed that fire was the basis of all life.

7. A good way to keep your trousers pressed is to hang them from the bureau drawer.

8. The chances are that you will never fill an inside straight.

9. The Republicans believe in a centralised government, the Democrats in a de-centralised one.

10. It is not necessarily effeminate to drink tea.

SENIOR YEAR

1. A dinner coat looks better than full dress.

2. There is as yet no law determining what constitutes trespass in an airplane.

3. Six hours of sleep are not necessary.

4. Bicarbonate of soda taken before retiring makes you feel better the next day.

5. You needn't be fully dressed if you wear a cap and gown to a nine-o'clock recitation.

6. Theatre tickets may be charged.

7. Flowers may be charged.

8. May is the shortest month in the year.

The foregoing outline of my education is true enough in its way, and is what people like to think about a college course. It has become quite the cynical thing to admit laughingly that college did one no good. It is part of the American Credo that all that the college student learns is to catch punts and dance. I had to write something like that to satisfy the editors. As a matter of fact, I learned a great deal in college and have those four years to thank for whatever I know to-day.

(The above note was written to satisfy those of my instructors and financial backers who may read this. As a matter of fact, the original outline is true, and I had to look up the date about Charlemagne at that.)

Fascinating Crimes

The Missing Floor

IT has often been pointed out that murderers are given to revisiting the scene of their crimes. The case of Edny Pastelle is the only one on record where the scene of the crime revisited the murderer.

Edny Pastelle was a Basque elevator woman who ran one of the first elevators installed in the old Fifth Avenue Hotel, which stood at the corner of Twenty-third Street and Fifth Avenue, New York City. The elevator was of the surrey type, and was pushed from floor to floor by the operator, who was underneath climbing on a ladder. It was Mlle. Pastelle's daily task to hoist such personages as Chauncey M. Depew, Boss Tweed and Harriet Beecher Stowe up to their rooms in the Fifth Avenue Hotel. In fact, she is said to have been Miss Stowe's model for *Uncle Tom* in the novel of that name (with the word " Cabin " added to it).

In the evenings, when Edny Pastelle was not on duty, she carried Punch and Judy shows about town for whoever wanted them. As not many people wanted them, Edny's evenings were pretty much her own.

The evening of July 7, 1891, however, is on record as being not Edny's, but Max Sorgossen's.

Max Sorgossen worked in the Eden Musée, which was situated on Twenty-third Street just below the Fifth Avenue Hotel. His job was to put fresh cuffs on the wax figure of Chester A. Arthur in the Presidential Group. At five o'clock every afternoon he also took " Ajeeb," the mechanical chess player, out in the back yard for his exercise.

At five-thirty on the afternoon in question Max Sorgossen had just knocked off work and was strolling up Twenty-third Street in search of diversion. In the back of his mind was an idea that perhaps he might find another mechanical chess player for " Ajeeb " and a girl for himself and that the four of them might go down to Coney Island for the evening, as the weather was warm. As he passed the service entrance of the Fifth Avenue Hotel he met Edny Pastelle, who was likewise calling it a day. (She called it a *jour*, but that is the Basque of it.)

Edny and Max had known each other in finishing school, and so there seemed no impropriety in his speaking to her and asking her if she knew of a mechanical chess player for " Ajeeb " and if she would look with favour on an evening at Coney.

The two were seen entering a restaurant on Twenty-first Street to talk it over at 6.10. At 9.20 the next morning guests of the hotel, on trying to descend in the elevator, found it stuck between the first and third floors. When the car was finally dislodged, it was found to contain the body of Max Sorgossen. Furthermore, *the second floor, where the elevator should have stopped, was gone.*

Edny Pastelle and Max Sorgossen in the gallery of human fiends and their victims.

—Courtesy of John Held, Jr., and Life.

47

Edny was arrested and the trial took place in the Court of Domestic Relations, since she was a domestic and there had evidently been relations, albeit unfriendly. The prosecuting attorney was a young lawyer named William T. Jerome, later William Travers Jerome. Following is a transcript of the cross-examination :

Q. What did you do after Sorgossen spoke to you on Twenty-third Street ?

A. Pardon.

Q. What did you do after Sorgossen spoke to you on Twenty-first Street ?

A. Plenty.

Q. Very good, Mr. Bones. And now tell me, why *is* a man with a silk hat on like Mary Queen of Scots ?

A. What Scots ?

Q. I'm asking *you*.

A. Animal, vegetable or mineral ?

Q. Mineral.

A. The tidy on the back of that chair ?

Q. No.

A. Cyrus W. Field ?

Q. Give up ?

A. Three spades.

Q. Double three spades.

At this point, counsel for the defence objected and the case was thrown out into a higher court, where Edny Pastelle was acquitted, or whatever you call it.

It was some thirty years later that the missing second floor of the old Fifth Avenue Hotel was discovered. A workman laying wagers on the sixteenth floor of the Fifth Avenue Building (erected on the site of the old Fifth Avenue Hotel) came across a floor which was neither the fifteenth, sixteenth nor seventeenth. The police were called in and, after several weeks of investigation and grilling, it was identified as the missing floor of the old hotel, the floor at which the little romance of Edny Pastelle had come to such an abrupt end. How it came to be on the sixteenth floor of the Fifth Avenue Building nobody knows. Perhaps Max Sorgossen could tell.

The Tooth, the Whole Tooth, and Nothing but the Tooth

SOME well-known saying (it doesn't make much difference what) is proved by the fact that everyone likes to talk about his experiences at the dentist's. For years and years little articles like this have been written on the subject, little jokes like some that I shall presently make have been made, and people in general have been telling other people just what emotions they experience when they crawl into the old red plush guillotine.

They like to explain to each other how they feel when the dentist puts " that buzzer thing " against their bicuspids, and, if sufficiently pressed, they will describe their sensations on mouthing a rubber dam.

" I'll tell you what I hate," they will say with great relish, " when he takes that little nut-pick and begins to scrape. Ugh ! "

" Oh, I'll tell you what's worse than that," says the friend, not to be outdone, " when he is poking around careless-like, and strikes a nerve. Wow ! "

And if there are more than two people at the experience-meeting, everyone will chip in and tell what he or she considers to be the worst phase of the dentist's work, all present enjoying the narration hugely and none so much as the narrator who has suffered so.

This sort of thing has been going on ever since the first mammoth gold tooth was hung out as a bait to folks in search of a good time. (By the way, when *did* the present obnoxious system of dentistry begin ? It can't be so very long ago that the electric auger was invented, and where would a dentist be without an electric auger ? Yet you never hear of Amalgam Filling Day, or any other anniversary in the dental year. There must be a conspiracy of silence on the part of the trade to keep hidden the names of the men who are responsible for all this.)

However many years it may be that dentists have been plying their trade, in all that time people have never tired of talking about their teeth. This is probably due to the inscrutable workings of Nature who is always supplying new teeth to talk about.

As a matter of fact, the actual time and suffering in the chair is only a fraction of the gross expenditure connected with the affair. The preliminary period, about which nobody talks, is much the worse. This dates from the discovery of the wayward tooth and extends to the moment when the dentist places his foot on the automatic hoist which jacks you up into range. Giving gas for tooth-extraction is all very humane in its way, but the time for anaesthetics is when the patient first decides that he must go to the dentist. From then on, until the first excavation is started, should be shrouded in oblivion.

There is probably no moment more appalling than that in which the tongue, running idly over the teeth in a moment of care-free play, comes suddenly upon the ragged edge of a space from which the old familiar filling has disappeared. The world stops and you look meditatively up to the corner of the ceiling. Then quickly you draw your tongue away, and try to laugh the affair off, saying to yourself :

" Stuff and nonsense, my good fellow ! There is nothing the matter with your tooth. Your nerves are upset after a hard day's work, that's all."

Having decided this to your satisfaction, you slyly, and with a poor attempt at being casual, slide the tongue back along the line of adjacent teeth, hoping against hope that it will reach the end without mishap.

But there it is ! There can be no doubt about it this time. The tooth simply has got to be filled by someone, and the only person who can fill it with anything permanent is a dentist. You wonder if you might not be able to patch it up yourself for the time being— a year or so—perhaps with a little spruce-gum and a coating of new-skin. It is fairly far back, and wouldn't have to be a very sightly job.

But this has an impracticable sound, even to you. You might want to eat some peanut-brittle (you never can tell when someone might offer you peanut-brittle these days), and the new-skin, while serviceable enough in the case of cream soups and custards, couldn't be expected to stand up under heavy crunching.

So you admit that, since the thing has got to be filled, it might as well be a dentist who does the job.

This much decided, all that is necessary is to call him up and make an appointment.

Let us say that this resolve is made on Tuesday. That afternoon you start to look up the dentist's number in the telephone book. A great wave of relief sweeps over you when you discover that it isn't there. How can you be expected to make an appointment with a man who hasn't got a telephone ? And how can you have a tooth filled without making an appointment ? The whole thing is impossible, and that's all there is to it. God knows you did your best.

On Wednesday there is a slightly more insistent twinge, owing to bad management of a sip of ice water. You decide that you simply must get in touch with that dentist when you get back from lunch. But you know how those things are. First one thing and then another came up, and a man came in from Providence who had to be shown around the office, and by the time you had a minute to yourself it was five o'clock. And, anyway, the tooth didn't bother you again. You wouldn't be surprised if, by being careful, you could get along with it as it is until the end of the week when you will have more time. A man has to think of his business, after all, and what is a little personal discomfort in the shape of an unfilled tooth to the satisfaction of work well done in the office ?

By Saturday morning you are fairly reconciled to going ahead, but it is only a half day and probably he has no appointments left, anyway. Monday is really the time. You can begin the week afresh. After all, Monday is really the logical day to start in going to the dentist.

Bright and early Monday morning you make another try at the telephone book, and find, to your horror, that some time between now and last Tuesday the dentist's name and number have been inserted into the directory. There it is. There is no getting around it: "Burgess, Jas. Kendal, DDS. . . . Courtland—2654." There is really nothing left to do but to call him up. Fortunately the line is busy, which gives you a perfectly good excuse for putting it over until Tuesday. But on Tuesday luck is against you and you get a clear connection with the doctor himself. An appointment is arranged for Thursday afternoon at 3.30.

Thursday afternoon, and here it is only Tuesday morning! Almost anything may happen between now and then. We might declare war on Mexico, and off you'd have to go, dentist appointment or no dentist appointment. Surely a man couldn't let a date to have a tooth filled stand in the way of his doing his duty to his country. Or the social revolution might start on Wednesday, and by Thursday the whole town might be in ashes. You can picture yourself standing, Thursday afternoon at 3.30, on the ruins of the City Hall, fighting off marauding bands of reds, and saying to yourself, with a sigh of relief: " Only to think ! At this time I was to have been climbing into the dentist's chair ! " You never can tell when your luck will turn in a thing like that.

But Wednesday goes by and nothing happens. And Thursday morning dawns without even a word from the dentist saying that he has been called suddenly out of town to lecture before the Incisor Club. Apparently, everything is working against you.

By this time, your tongue has taken up a permanent resting place in the vacant tooth, and is causing you to talk indistinctly and incoherently. Somehow you feel that if the dentist opens your mouth and finds the tip of your tongue in the tooth, he will be deceived and go away without doing anything.

The only thing left is for you to call him up and say that you have just killed a man and are being arrested and can't possibly keep your appointment. But any dentist would see through that. He would laugh right into his transmitter at you. There is probably no excuse which it would be possible to invent which a dentist has not already heard eighty or ninety times. No, you might as well see the thing through now.

Luncheon is a ghastly rite. The whole left side of your jaw has suddenly developed an acute sensitiveness and the disaffection has spread to the four teeth on either side of the original one. You doubt if it will be possible for him to touch it at all. Perhaps all he intends to do this time is to look at it anyway. You might even suggest that to him. You could very easily come in again soon and have him do the actual work.

Three-thirty draws near. A horrible time of day at best. Just when a man's vitality is lowest. Before stepping in out of the sunlight into the building in which the dental parlour is, you take one look about you at the happy people scurrying by in the street. Carefree children that they are! What do they know of Life? Probably that man in the silly-looking hat never had trouble with so much as his baby teeth. There they go, pushing and jostling each other, just as if within ten feet of them there was not a man who stands on the brink of the Great Misadventure. Ah well! Life is like that!

Into the elevator. The last hope is gone. The door clangs and you look hopelessly about you at the stupid faces of your fellow passengers. How can people be so clownish? Of course, there is always the chance that the elevator will fall and that you will all be terribly hurt. But that is too much to expect. You dismiss it from your thoughts as too impractical, too visionary. Things don't work out as happily as that in real life.

You feel a certain glow of heroic pride when you tell the operator the right floor number. You might just as easily have told him a floor too high or too low, and that would, at least, have caused delay. But after all, a man must prove himself a man and the least you can do is to meet Fate with an unflinching eye and give the right floor number.

Too often has the scene in the dentist's waiting room been described for me to try to do it again here. They are all alike. The antiseptic smell, the ominous hum from the operating rooms, the ancient *Digests*, and the silent, sullen group of waiting patients, each trying to look unconcerned and cordially disliking everyone else in the room—all these have been sung by poets of far greater lyric powers than mine. (Not that I really think that they *are* greater than mine, but that's the customary form of excuse for not writing something you haven't got time or space to do. As a matter of fact, I think I could do it much better than it has ever been done before.)

I can only say that, as you sit looking, with unseeing eyes, through a large book entitled, "The War in Pictures," you would gladly change places with the most lowly of God's creatures. It is inconceivable that there should be anyone worse off than you, unless perhaps it is some of the poor wretches who are waiting with you.

That one over in the arm-chair, nervously tearing to shreds a copy of "The Dental Review and Practical Inlay Worker." She may have something frightful the trouble with her. She couldn't possibly look more worried. Perhaps it is very, very painful. This thought cheers you up considerably. What cowards women are in times like these!

And then there comes the sound of voices from the next room.

"All right, Doctor, and if it gives me any more pain shall I call you up? . . . Do you think that it will bleed much more? . . . Saturday morning, then, at eleven. . . . Good bye, Doctor."

And a middle-aged woman emerges (all women are middle-aged

when emerging from the dentist's office) looking as if she were playing the big emotional scene in " John Ferguson." A wisp of hair waves dissolutely across her forehead between her eyes. Her face is pale, except for a slight inflammation at the corners of her mouth, and in her eyes is that far-away look of one who has been face to face with Life. But she is through. She should care how she looks.

The nurse appears, and looks inquiringly at each one in the room. Each one in the room evades the nurse's glance in one last, futile attempt to fool someone and get away without seeing the dentist. But she spots you and nods pleasantly. God, how pleasantly she nods ! There ought to be a law against people being as pleasant as that.

" The doctor will see you now," she says.

The English language may hold a more disagreeable combination of words than " The doctor will see you now." I am willing to concede something to the phrase " Have you anything to say before the current is turned on." That may be worse for the moment, but it doesn't last so long. For continued, unmitigating depression, I know nothing to equal " The doctor will see you now." But I'm not narrow-minded about it. I'm willing to consider other possibilities.

Smiling feebly, you trip over the extended feet of the man next to you, and stagger into the delivery room, where amid a ghastly array of death masks of teeth, blue flames waving eerily from Bunsen burners, and the drowning sound of perpetually running water which chokes and gurgles at intervals, you sink into the chair and close your eyes.

$$* \qquad * \qquad * \qquad * \qquad *$$

But now let us consider the spiritual exaltation that comes when you are at last let down and turned loose. It is all over, and what did it amount to ? Why, nothing at all. A-ha-ha-ha-ha-ha ! Nothing at all.

You suddenly develop a particular friendship for the dentist. A splendid fellow, really. You ask him questions about his instruments. What does he use this thing for, for instance ? Well, well, to think of a little thing like that making all that trouble. A-ha-ha-ha-ha-ha ! . . . And the dentist's family, how are they ? Isn't that fine !

Gaily you shake hands with him and straighten your tie. Forgotten is the fact that you have another appointment with him for Monday. There is no such thing as Monday. You are through for to-day, and all's right with the world.

As you pass out through the waiting room, you leer at the others unpleasantly. The poor fishes ! Why can't they take their medicine like grown people and not sit there moping as if they were going to be shot ?

Heigh-ho! Here's the elevator man! A charming fellow! You wonder if he knows that you have just had a tooth filled. You feel tempted to tell him and slap him on the back. You feel tempted to tell everyone out in the bright, cheery street. And what a wonderful street it is too! All full of nice, black snow and water. After all, Life is sweet!

And then you go and find the first person whom you can accost without being arrested and explain to him just what it was that the dentist did to you, and how you felt, and what you have got to have done next time.

Which brings us right back to where we were in the beginning, and perhaps accounts for everyone's liking to divulge their dental secrets to others. It may be a sort of hysterical relief that, for the time being, it is all over with.

The Boys' Camp Business

THERE seems to be an idea prevalent among parents that a good way to solve the summer problem for the boy is to send him to a boys' camp. At any rate, the idea seems to be prevalent in the advertising pages of the magazines.

If all the summer camps for boys and girls turn out the sterling citizens-in-embryo that they claim to do, the future of this country is as safe as if it were in the hands of a governing board consisting of the Twelve Apostles. From the folders and advertisements, we learn that " Camp Womagansett—in the foothills of the White Mountains " sends yearly into the world a bevy of " strong, manly boys, ready for the duties of citizenship and equipped to face life with a clear eye and a keen mind." It doesn't say anything about their digestions, but I suppose they are in tiptop shape, too.

The outlook for the next generation of mothers is no less dazzling. " Camp Wawilla for Girls," we learn, pays particular attention to the spiritual development of To-morrow's Women and compared to the civic activities of the majority of alumnæ of Wawilla, those of Florence Nightingale or Frances Willard would have to be listed under the head of " Junior Girls' Work."

Now this is all very splendid, and it is comforting to think that when every boy and girl goes to Womagansett or Wawilla there will be no more Younger Generation problem and probably no crime waves worth mentioning. But there are several other features that go hand in hand with sending the boy to camp which I would like to take up from the parents' point of view, if I may. I will limit myself to twenty minutes.

In the first place, when your boy comes home from camp he is what is known in the circular as "manly and independent." This means that when you go swimming with him he pushes you off the raft and jumps on your shoulders, holding you under water until you are as good as drowned—better, in fact. Before he went to

" Now watch Daddy. See ? Hands like this, bend your knees. See ? "

camp, you used to take a kindly interest in his swimming and tell him to "take your time, take it easy," with a feeling of superiority which, while it may have had no foundation in your own natatorial prowess, nevertheless was one of the few points of pride left to you in your obese middle-age. After watching one of those brown heroes in one-piece suits and rubber helmets dive off a tower and swim under water to the raft and back, there was a sort of balm in being able to turn to your son and show him how to do the crawl stroke, even though you yourself weren't one of the seven foremost crawl experts in the country. You could do it better than your son could, and that was something.

It was also very comforting to be able to stand on the springboard and say : " Now watch Daddy. See ? Hands like this, bend your knees. See ? " The fact that such exhibitions usually culminated in your landing heavily on the area bounded by the knees and the chest was embarrassing, perhaps, but at that you weren't quite so bad as the boy when he tried the same thing.

But after a summer at camp, the " manly, independent " boy comes back and makes you look like Horace Greeley in his later years. " Do this one, Dad ! " he says, turning a double flip off the spring-board and cutting into the water like a knife blade. If you try it, you sprain your back. If you don't try it, your self-respect and prestige are shattered. The best thing to do is not to hear him. You can do this by disappearing under the surface every time it looks as if he were going to pull a new one. After a while, however, this ruse gets you pretty soggy and waterlogged and you might better just go in and get dressed as rapidly as possible.

The worst phase of this new-found " independence " is the romping instinct that seems to be developed to a high state of obnoxiousness at all boys' camps. I went to camp when I was a boy, but I don't remember being as unpleasant about my fun as boys to-day seem to be. I have done many mean things in my time. I have tortured flies and kicked crutches out from under cripples' arms. But I have never, so help me, Confucius, pushed anybody off a raft or come up behind anyone in the water and jumped up on his shoulders. And I don't think that Lincoln ever did, either.

There is evidently a course in raft pushing and back jumping in boys' camps to-day. Those photographs that you see in the camp advertisements, if you examine them closely, will disclose, in nine cases out of ten, a lot of boys pushing each other off rafts. You can't see the ones who are jumping on others' shoulders, as they are under water. But I want to serve notice right now that the next boy who pushes me off a raft when I am not looking, or tries to play leapfrog over me in ten feet of water, is going to be made practically useless as To-morrow's Citizen, and I am going to do it myself, too. If it happens to be my own son, it will just make the affair the sadder.

Another thing that these manly boys learn at camp is a savage habit of getting up at sunrise. The normal, healthy boy should be a very late sleeper. Who does not remember in his own normal, healthy boyhood having to be called three, four, or even five times in the morning before it seemed sensible to get up ? One of the happiest memories of childhood is that of the maternal voice calling up from downstairs, fading away into silence, and the realisation that it would be possibly fifteen minutes before it called again.

All this is denied to the boy who goes to a summer camp. When he comes home, he is so steeped in the pernicious practice of early rising that he can't shake it off. Along about six o'clock in the morning he begins dropping shoes and fixing up a new stand for the radio in his room. Then he goes out into the back yard and practices tennis shots up against the house. Then he runs over a few whistling arrangements of popular songs and rides his bicycle up and down the gravel path. You would be surprised at the sound two bicycle wheels can make on a gravel path at six-thirty in the

You'd be surprised at the sound two bicycle wheels can make on a gravel path.

morning. A forest fire might make the same crackling sound, but you probably wouldn't be having a forest fire out in your yard at six-thirty in the morning. Not if you had any sense, you wouldn't.

Just what the boys do at camp when they get up at six is a mystery. They seem to have some sort of setting-up exercises and a swim—more pushing each other off the raft—but they could do that by getting up at eight and still have a good long day ahead of them. I never knew anyone yet who got up at six who did anything more useful between that time and breakfast than banging a tennis ball up against the side of the house, waiting for the civilised members of the party to get up. We have to do enough waiting in this life without getting up early to wait for breakfast.

Next summer I have a good mind to run a boys' camp of my own. It will be on Lake Chabonagogchabonagogchabonagungamog—yes, there is, too, in Webster, Massachusetts—and I will call it Camp Chabonagogchabonagogchabonagungamog for Manly Boys. And by the word " manly," I will mean " like men." In other words, everyone shall sleep just as long as he wants, and when he does get up there will be no depleting " setting-up " exercises. The day will be spent just as the individual camper gosh-darned pleases. No organised " hikes "—I'd like a word on the " hike " problem some day, too—no camp spirit, no talk about To-morrow's Manhood, and *no pushing people off rafts.*

The Passing of the Orthodox Paradox

WHATEVER irreparable harm may have been done to Society by the recent epidemic of crook, sex and other dialect plays, one great alleviation has resulted. They have driven up-stage, for the time being, the characters who exist on tea and repartee in " The drawing room of Sir Arthur Peaversham's town house, Grosvenor Square. Time : late Autumn."

A person in a crook play may have talked underworld patois which no self-respecting criminal would have allowed himself to utter, but he did not sit on a divan and evolve abnormal *bons mots* with each and every breath. The misguided and misinformed daughter in the Self and Sex Play may have lisped words which only an internee should hear, but she did not offer a succession of brilliant but meaningless paradoxes as a substitute for real conversation.

" *Snappy back-talk is now encountered chiefly in such acts as 'Cooney &*
Le Blanc, the Eccentric Comedy Dancing Team.' "

Continuously snappy back-talk is now encountered chiefly in such acts as those of " Cooney & LeBlanc, the Eccentric Comedy Dancing Team." And even *they* manage to scrape along without the paradoxes.

But there was a time, beginning with the Oscar Wilde era, when no unprotected thought was safe. It might be seized at any moment by an English Duke or a Lady Agatha and strangled to death. Even the butlers in the late 'eighties were wits, and served epigrams with cucumber sandwiches ; and a person entering one of these drawing rooms and talking in connected sentences—easily understood by everybody—each with one subject, predicate and meaning, would have been looked upon as a high-class moron. One might as well have gone to a dinner at Lady Coventry's without one's collar, as without one's kit of trained paradoxes.

A late Autumn afternoon in one of these semi-Oscar Wilde plays, for instance, would run something like this :

SCENE—*The Octagon Room in Lord Raymond Eaveston's Manor House in Stropshire.*

LADY EAVESTON *and* SIR THOMAS WAFFLETON *are discovered, arranging red flowers in a vase.*

SIR T.: I detest red flowers ; they are so yellow.

LADY E.: What a cynic you are, Sir Thomas. I really must not listen to you or I shall hear something that you say.

SIR T.: Not at all, my dear Lady Eaveston. I detest people who listen closely ; they are so inattentive.

LADY E.: Pray do not be analytical, my dear Sir Thomas. When people are extremely analytical with me I am sure that they are superficial, and, to me, nothing is more abominable than superficiality, unless perhaps it is an intolerable degree of thoroughness.

(*Enter Meadows, the Butler*)

MEADOWS (*announcing*) : Sir Mortimer Longley and Mrs. Wrennington—a most remarkable couple—I may say in announcing them—in that there is nothing at all remarkable about them.

(*Enter Sir Mortimer and Mrs. Wrennington*)

MRS. W.: So sorry to be late, dear Lady Eaveston. But it is so easy to be on time that I always make it a point to be late. It lends poise, and poise is a charming quality for any woman to have, am I not right, Sir Thomas ?

SIR T.: You are always right, my dear Mrs. Wrennington, and never more so than now, for I know of no more attractive attribute than poise, unless perhaps it be embarrassment.

LADY E.: What horrid cynics you men are ! Really, Sir Thomas, one might think, from your sophisticated remarks that you had been brought up in the country and had seen nothing of life.

SIR T.: And so I *have* been, my dear Lady Eaveston. To my mind, London is nothing but the country, and certainly Stropshire is nothing but a metropolis. The difference is, that when one is in town, one lives with others, and when one is in the country, others live with one. And both plans are abominable.

MRS. W.: What a horrid combination ! I hate horrid combinations ; they always turn out to be so extremely pleasant.

(*Enter Meadows*)

MEADOWS (*announcing*) : Sir Roland Pinshamton ; Viscount Lemingham ; Countess Trotski and Mr. Peters. In announcing these parties I cannot refrain from remarking that it has always been my opinion that a man who intends to get married should either know something or nothing, preferably both.

(*Exit Meadows*)

" The butler served epigrams with the cucumber sandwiches."

COUNTESS T.: So sorry to be late, my dear Lady Eaveston. It was charmingly tolerant of you to have us.

LADY E.: Invitations are never tolerant, my dear Countess; acceptances always are. But do tell me, how is your husband, the Count—or perhaps he is no longer your husband. One never knows these days whether a man is his wife's husband or whether she is simply his wife.

COUNTESS T. (*lighting a cigarette*): Really, Lady Eaveston, you grow more and more interesting. I detest interesting people; they are so hopelessly uninteresting. It is like beautiful people—who are usually so singularly unbeautiful. Has not that been your experience, Sir Mortimer?

SIR M.: May I have the pleasure of escorting you to the music room, Mrs. Wrennington?

(*Exeunt omnes to music room for dinner*)

Curtain.

It is from this that we have, in a measure, been delivered by th court room scenes, and all the medical dramas. But the paradox still remains intrenched in English writing behind Mr. G. K. Chesterton, and he may be considered, by literary tacticians, as considerable stronghold.

Here again we find our commonplaces shaken up until they emerge in what looks like a new and tremendously imposing shape, and all of them ostensibly proving the opposite of what we have always understood. If we do not quite catch the precise meaning at first reading, we lay it to our imperfect perception and try to do better on the next one. It seldom occurs to us that it really may have no meaning at all and never was intended to have any, any more than the act of hanging by your feet from parallel bars has any further significance than that you can manage to do it.

So before retiring to the privacy of our personal couches, let us thank an all wise Providence, that the drama paradox has passed away.

The
Last Day

WHEN, during the long winter evenings, you sit around the snapshot album and recall the merry, merry times you had on your vacation, there is one day which your memory mercifully overlooks. It is the day you packed up and left the summer resort to go home.

This Ultimate Day really begins the night before, when you sit up until one o'clock trying to get things into the trunks and bags. This is when you discover the well-known fact that summer air swells articles to twice or three times their original size; so that the sneakers which in June fitted in between the phonograph and the book (which you have never opened), in September are found to require a whole tray for themselves and even then one of them will probably have to be carried in the hand.

Along about midnight, the discouraging process begins to get on your nerves and you snap at your wife and she snaps at you every time it is found that something won't fit in the suitcase. As you have both gradually dispensed with the more attractive articles of clothing under stress of the heat and the excitement, these little word passages take on the sordid nature of a squabble in an East Side tenement, and all that is needed is for one of the children to wake up and start whimpering. This it does.

It is finally decided that there is no sense in trying to finish the job that night. General nervousness, combined with a specific fear of oversleeping, results in a troubled tossing of perhaps three hours in bed, and ushers in the dawn of the last day on just about as irritable and bleary-eyed a little family as you will find outside an institution.

The trouble starts right away with the process of getting dressed in travelling clothes which haven't been worn since the trip up. Junior's shoulders are still tender, and he decides that it will be impossible for him to wear his starched blouse. One of Philip's good shoes, finding that there has been no call for it during the summer, has become hurt and has disappeared; so Philip has to wear a pair of Daddy's old bathing shoes which had been thrown away. (After everything has been locked and taken out of the room the good shoe is found in the closet and left for dead.)

You, yourself, aren't any too successful in reverting to city clothes. Several weeks of soft collars and rubber-soled shoes have softened you to a point where the old " Deroy-14½ " feels like a napkin ring around your neck, and your natty brogans are so heavy that you lose your balance and topple over forward if you step out suddenly. The whole effect of your civilian costume when surveyed in a mirror is that of a Maine guide all dressed up for an outing " up to Bangor."

Incidentally, it shapes up as one of the hottest days of the season —or any other season.

" Oh, look how funny Daddy looks in his straw hat ! "

" I never realised before, Fred, how much too high the crown is for the length of your face. Are you sure it's your hat ? "

" It's my hat, all right," is the proper reply, " but maybe the face belongs to somebody else."

This silences them for a while, but on and off during the day a lot of good-natured fun is had in calling the attention of outsiders to the spectacle presented by Daddy in his " store " clothes.

Once everyone is dressed, there must be an excursion to take one last look at the ocean, or lake, or whatever particular prank of Nature it may have been which has served as an inducement to you to leave the city. This must be done before breakfast. So down to the beach you go, getting your shoes full of sand, and wait while Sister, in a sentimental attempt to feel the water for the last time, has tripped and fallen in, soaking herself to the garters. There being no dry clothes left out, she has to go in the kitchen and stand in front of the stove until at least one side of her is dry.

Breakfast bears no resemblance to any other meal eaten in the place. There is a poorly suppressed feeling that you must hurry, coupled with the stiff collar and tight clothes, which makes it practically impossible to get any food down past the upper chest.

Then follows one of the worst features of the worst of all vacation days—the good-byes. It isn't that you hate to part company with these people. They too, as they stand there in their summer clothes, seem to have undergone some process whereby you see them as they really are and not as they seemed when you were all together up to your necks in water or worrying a tennis ball back and forth over a net. And you may be sure that you, in your town clothes, seem doubly unattractive to them.

Here is Mrs. Tremble, who lives in Montclair, N.J., in the winter. That really is a terrible hat of hers, now that you get a good look at it. " Well, good-bye, Mrs. Tremble. Be sure to look us up if you ever get out our way. We are right in the telephone book, and we'll have a regular get-together meeting. . . . Good-bye, Marian. Think of us to-night in the hot city, and be sure to let us know when you are going through. . . . Well, so long, Mr. Prothero ; look out for those girls up at the post office. Don't let any of them marry you. . . . Well, we're off, Mrs. Rostetter. Yes, we're leaving to-day. On the 10.45. We have to be back for Junior's school. It begins on the 11th. *Good*-bye ! "

It is then found that there is about an hour to wait before the machine comes to take you to the station ; so all the good-byes have been wasted and have to be gone through with again.

In the meantime, Mother decides that she must run over to the Bide-a-Wee cottage and say good-bye to the Sisbys. The children feel that they are about due for another last look at the ocean. And Daddy remembers that he hasn't been able to shut the big suitcase yet. So the family disperses in various directions and each unit gets lost. Mother, rushing out from the Sisby's in a panic thinking that she hears the automobile, is unable to find the others. Little Mildred, having taken it upon herself to look out for the other children while they are gazing on the ocean, has felt it incumbent on her to spank Philip for trying to build one last tunnel in the sand, resulting in a bitter physical encounter in which Philip easily batters his sister into a state of hysteria. Daddy, having wilted his collar and put his knee through his straw hat in an attempt to jam the suitcase together, finds that the thing can't be done and takes out the box of sea shells that Junior had planned to take home for his cabinet, and hides them under the bed.

The suitcase at last having been squeezed shut and placed with the rest of the bags in the hall, the maid comes running up with five damp bathing suits which she has found hanging on the line and wants to know if they belong here. Daddy looks cautiously down the hall and whispers : " No ! "

Looks cautiously down the hall and whispers : " No ! "

At last the automobile arrives and stands honking by the roadside. "Come, Junior, quick, put your coat on ! . . . Have you got the bag with the thermos ? . . . Hurry, Philip ! . . . Where's Sister ? . . . Come, Sister ! . . . Well, it's too late now. You'll have to wait till we get on the train . . . Good-bye, Mrs. Tremble . . . Be sure to look us up . . . Good-bye, everybody ! . . . Here,

Junior! Put that down! You can't take that with you. No, no! That belongs to that other little boy . . . *Junior!* . . . Good-bye, Marian! . . . Good-bye, Mrs. McNerdle! . . . Philip, say good-bye to Mrs. McNerdle, she's been so good to you, don't you remember? . . . Good-bye, Mrs. McNerdle, that's right. . . . *Good-bye!* "

And with that the automobile starts, the friends on the porch wave and call out indistinguishable pleasantries, Junior begins to cry, and it is found that Ed has no hat.

The trip home in the heat and cinders is enlivened by longing reminiscences : "Well, it's eleven o'clock. I suppose they're all getting into their bathing suits now. How'd you like to jump into that old ocean right this minute, eh?" (As a matter of fact, the speaker has probably not been induced to go into "that old ocean" more than three times during the whole summer.)

The fact that they reach home too late to get a regular dinner and have to go to bed hungry, and the more poignant impressions in the process of opening a house which has been closed all summer, have all been treated of before in an article called "The Entrance Into the Tomb." And so we will leave our buoyant little family, their vacation ended, all ready to jump into the swing of their work, refreshed, invigorated, and clear-eyed.

Looking Shakespeare Over

AT the end of the current theatrical season, the trustees of the Shakespeare estate will probably get together at the Stratford House and get pie-eyed. It has been a banner year for "the Immortal Bard," as his wife used to call him. Whatever the royalties are that revert to the estate, there will be enough to buy a couple of rounds anyway, and maybe enough left over to hire an entertainer.

There was a time during the winter in New York when you couldn't walk a block without stepping on some actor or actress playing Shakespeare. They didn't all make money, but it got the author's name into the papers, and publicity never hurt anyone, let alone a writer who has been dead three hundred years and whose stuff isn't adaptable for the movies.

The only trouble with acting Shakespeare is the actors. It brings out the worst that is in them. A desire to read aloud the soliloquy (you know the one I mean) is one of the first symptoms a man has that he is going to be an actor. If ever I catch any of my little boys going out behind the barn to recite this speech, I will take them right away to a throat specialist and have their palates emoved. One failure is enough in a family.

And then, too, the stuff that Will wrote, while all right to sit at home and read, does *not* lend itself to really snappy entertainment on the modern stage. It takes just about the best actor in the world to make it sound like anything more than a declamation by the young lady representing the Blue and the Grey on Memorial Day. I know that I run counter to many cultured minds in this matter, but I think that, if the truth were known, there are a whole lot more of us who twitch through two-thirds of a Shakespearean performance than the last census would lead one to believe. With a company consisting of one or two stars and the rest hams (which is a good liberal estimate) what can you expect? Even Shakespeare himself couldn't sit through it without reading the ads on the programme a little.

But you can't blame the actor entirely. According to present standards of what constitutes dramatic action, most of Will's little dramas have about as much punch as a reading of a treasurer's report. To be expected to thrill over the dramatic situations incident to a large lady's dressing up as a boy and fooling her own husband, or to follow breathlessly a succession of scenes strung together like magic-lantern slides and each ending with a perfectly corking rhymed couplet, is more than ought to be asked of anyone who has, in the same season, seen " Loyalties " or any one of the real plays now running on Broadway.

It is hard to ask an actor to make an exit on a line like :

> " I am glad on't : I desire no more delight
> Than to be under sail and gone to-night "

without sounding like one of the characters in Palmer Cox's Brownies saying :

> " And thus it was the Brownie Band,
> Came tumbling into Slumberland."

That is why they always have to exit laughingly in a Shakespearean production. The author has provided them with such rotten exits. If they don't do something—laugh, cry, turn a handspring, or something—they are left flat in the middle of the stage with nothing to do but say : " Well, I must be going." In " The Merchant of Venice," the characters are forced to keep up a running fire of false-sounding laughter to cover up the artificial nature of what they have just said :

" At the park gate, and therefore haste away
For we must measure twenty miles to-day. A-ha-ha-ha-ha-ha !"
   (*Off l. c.*)

To hear *Lorenzo* and *Gratiano* walking off together you would have thought that *Lorenzo* had the finest line of funny stories in all Venice, so loud and constantly did they laugh, whereas, if the truth were known, it was simply done to save their own and Shakespeare's face. Now my contention is that any author who can't get his stuff over on the stage without making the actors do contortions, is not

E   65 so good a playwright technically as Eugene Walters is. And now for the matter of comedy.

An actor, in order to get Shakespeare's comedy across, has got to roll his eyes, rub his stomach, kick his father in the seat, make his voice crack, and place his finger against the side of his nose. There is a great deal of talk about the vulgarity and slap-stick humour of the movies. If the movies ever tried to put anything over as horsy and crass as the scene in which young *Gobbo* kids his blind father, or *Falstaff* hides in the laundry hamper, there would be sermons preached on it in pulpits all over the country. It is impossible for a good actor, as we know good actors to-day, to handle a Shakespearean low comedy part, for it demands mugging and tricks which no good actor would permit himself to do. If Shakespeare were alive to-day and writing comedy for the movies, he would be the head-liner in the Mack Sennett studios. What he couldn't do with a cross-eyed man !

Another thing which has made the enjoyment of Shakespeare on the stage a precarious venture for this section of the theatre-going public at least, is the thoroughness with which the schools have desiccated his works. In " The Merchant of Venice," for example, there was hardly a line spoken which had not been so diagnosed by English teachers from the third grade up that it had lost every vestige of freshness and grace which it may once have had. Every time I changed schools, I ran into a class which was just taking up " The Merchant of Venice." Consequently, I learned to hate every word of the play. When *Bassanio* said :

" Which makes her seat of Belmont Colchis' strand,
And many Jasons come in quest of her "

in my mind there followed a chorus of memories of questions asked by Miss Mergatroid, Miss O'Shea, Miss Twitchell, Mr. Henby and Professor Greenally, such as : " Now what did Shakespeare mean by ' Colchis strand ' ? " " Can anyone in the room tell me why Portia's lovers were referred to as ' Jasons ' ? Robert Benchley, I wonder if you can leave off whispering to Harold Bemis long enough to tell me what other Portia in history is mentioned in this passage ? "

Perhaps that is the whole trouble with Shakespeare anyway. Too many people have taken him up. If they would let you alone, to read snatches from his plays now and then when you wanted to, and *stop* reading when you wanted to, it might not be so bad. But no ! They must ask you what he meant by this, and where the inflection should come on that, and they must stand up in front of scenery and let a lot of hams declaim at you while you are supposed to murmur " Gorgeous ! " and " How well he knew human nature ! " as if you couldn't go to Bartlett's " Quotations " and get the meat of it in half the time. I wouldn't be surprised, if things keep on as they are, if Shakespeare began to lose his hold on people. I give him ten centuries more at the outside.

Polyp with a Past

The Story of an Organism with a Heart

O F all forms of animal life, the polyp is probably the most neglected by fanciers. People seem willing to pay attention to anything, cats, lizards, canaries, or even fish, but simply because the polyp is reserved by nature and not given to showing off or wearing its heart on its sleeve, it is left alone under the sea to slave away at coral-building with never a kind word or a pat on the tentacles from anybody.

It was quite by accident that I was brought face to face with the human side of a polyp. I had been working on a thesis on " Emotional Crisis in Sponge Life," and came upon a polyp formation on a piece of coral in the course of my laboratory work. To say that I was astounded would be putting it mildly. I was surprised.

The difficulty in research work in this field came in isolating a single polyp from the rest in order to study the personal peculiarities of the little organism, for, as is so often the case (even, I fear, with us great big humans sometimes), the individual behaves in an entirely different manner in private from the one he adopts when there is a crowd around. And a polyp, among all creatures, has a minimum of time to himself in which to sit down and think. There is always a crowd of other polyps dropping in on him, urging him to make a fourth in a string of coral beads or just to come out and stick around on a rock for the sake of good fellowship.

The one which I finally succeeded in isolating was an engaging organism with a provocative manner and a little way of wrinkling up its ectoderm which put you at once at your ease. There could be no formality about your relations with this polyp five minutes after your first meeting. You were just like one great big family.

Although I have no desire to retail gossip, I think that readers of this treatise ought to be made aware of the fact (if, indeed, they do not already know it) that a polyp is really neither one thing nor another in matters of gender. One day it may be a little boy polyp, another day a little girl, according to its whim or practical considerations of policy. On grey days, when everything seems to be going wrong, it may decide that it will be neither boy nor girl but will just drift. I think that if we big human cousins of the little polyp were to follow the example set by these lowliest of God's creatures in this matter, we all would find ourselves much better off in the end. Am I not right, little polyp ?

What was my surprise, then, to discover my little friend one day in a gloomy and morose mood. It refused the peanut-butter which I had brought it and I observed through the microscope that it was shaking with sobs. Lifting it up with a pair of pincers I took it over to the window to let it watch the automobiles go by, a diversion which had, in the past, never failed to amuse. But I could see that it was not interested. A tune from the Victrola fell equally flat, even though I set my little charge on the centre of the disc and allowed it to revolve at a dizzy pace, which frolic usually sent it into spasms of excited giggling. Something was wrong. It was under emotional stress of the most racking kind.

I consulted Klunzinger's " Die Korallenthiere des Rothen Meeres " and there found that at an early age the polyp is quite likely to become the victim of a sentimental passion which is directed at its own self.

In other words, my tiny companion was in love with itself, bitterly, desperately, head-over-heels in love.

In an attempt to divert it from this madness, I took it on an extended tour of the Continent, visiting all the old cathedrals and stopping at none but the best hotels. The malady grew worse, instead of better. I thought that perhaps the warm sun of Granada would bring the colour back into those pale tentacles, but there the inevitable romance in the soft air was only fuel to the flame, and, in the shadow of the Alhambra, my little polyp gave up the fight and died of a broken heart without ever having declared its love to itself.

I returned to America shortly after not a little chastened by what I had witnessed of Nature's wonders in the realm of passion.

Paul Revere's Ride

How a Modest Go-Getter Did His Bit for the Juno Acid Bath Corporation

FOLLOWING are the salesman's report sheets sent into the home office in New York by Thaddeus Olin, agent for the Juno Acid Bath Corporation. Mr. Olin had the New England territory during the spring of 1775 and these report sheets are dated April 16, 17, 18 and 19, of that year.

April 16, 1775.
Boston.

Called on the following engravers this a.m.: Boston Engraving Co., E. H. Hosstetter, Theodore Platney, Paul Revere, Benjamin B. Ashley and Roger Durgin.

Boston Engraving Co. are all taken care of for their acid.

E. H. Hosstetter took three tins of acid No. 4 on trial and renewed his old order of 7 Queen-Biters.

Theodore Platney has gone out of business since my last trip.

Paul Revere was not in. The man in his shop said that he was busy with some sort of local shindig. Said I might catch him in to-morrow morning.

The Benjamin Ashley people said they were satisfied with their present product and contemplated no change.

Roger Durgin died last March.

Things are pretty quiet in Boston right now.

April 17.

Called on Boston Engraving people again to see if they might not want to try some Daisy No. 3. Mr. Lithgo was interested and said to come in to-morrow when Mr. Lithgo, Senior, would be there.

Paul Revere was not in. He had been in for a few minutes before the shop opened and had left word that he would be up at Sam Adams' in case anyone wanted him. Went up to the Adams place, but the girl there said that Mr. Revere and Mr. Adams had gone over to Mr. Dawes' place on Milk Street. Went to Dawes' place, but the man there said Dawes and Adams and Revere were in conference. There seems to be some sort of parade or something they are getting up, something to do with the opening of the new foot-bridge to Cambridge, I believe.

Things are pretty quiet here in Boston, except for the trade from the British fleet which is out in the harbour.

Spent the evening looking around in the coffee houses. Everyone here is cribbage-crazy. All they seem to think of is cribbage, cribbage, cribbage.

April 18.

To the Boston Engraving Company and saw Mr. Lithgo, Senior. He seemed interested in the Daisy No. 3 acid and said to drop in again later in the week.

Paul Revere was out. His assistant said that he knew that Mr. Revere was in need of a new batch of acid and had spoken to him about our Vulcan No. 2 and said he might try some. I would have to see Mr. Revere personally, he said, as Mr. Revere makes all purchases himself. He said that he thought I could catch him over at the Dawes' place.

Tried the Dawes' place but they said that he and Mr. Revere had gone over to the livery stable on State Street.

Went to the livery stable but Revere had gone. They said he had engaged a horse for to-night for some sort of entertainment he was taking part in. The hostler said he heard Mr. Revere say to Mr. Dawes that they might as well go up to the North Church and see if everything was all set; so I gather it is a church entertainment.

Followed them up to the North Church, but there was nobody there except the caretaker, who said that he thought I could catch Mr. Revere over at Charlestown late that night. He described him to me so that I would know him and said that he probably would be on horseback. As it seemed to me to be pretty important that we land the Revere order for Vulcan No. 2, I figured out that whatever inconvenience it might cause me to go over to Charlestown or whatever added expense to the firm, would be justified.

Spent the afternoon visiting several printing establishments, but none of them do any engraving.

Things are pretty quiet here in Boston.

Went over to Charlestown after supper and hung around " The Bell in Hand " tavern looking for Mr. Revere. Met a man there who used to live in Peapack, N.J., and we got to talking about what a funny name for a town that was. Another man said that in Massachusetts there was actually a place called Podunk, up near Worcester. We had some very good cheese and talked over names of towns for a while. Then the second man, the one who knew about Podunk, said he had to go as he had a date with a man. After he had left I happened to bring the conversation around to the fact that I was waiting for a Mr. Paul Revere, and the first man told me that I had been talking to him for half an hour and that he had just gone.

I rushed out to the corner, but the man who keeps the watering trough there said that someone answering Mr. Revere's description had just galloped off on a horse in the direction of Medford. Well, this just made me determined to land that order for Juno Acid Bath Corporation or die in the attempt. So I hired a horse at the Tavern stable and started off toward Medford.

Just before I hit Medford I saw a man standing out in his night-shirt in front of his house looking up the road. I asked him if he had seen anybody who looked like Mr. Revere. He seemed pretty sore and said that some crazy coot had just ridden by and knocked at his door and yelled something that he couldn't understand and that if he caught him he'd break his back. From his description of the horse I gathered that Mr. Revere was the man ; so I galloped on.

A lot of people in Medford Town were up and standing in front of their houses, cursing like the one I had just seen. It seems that Mr. Revere had gone along the roadside, knocking on doors and yelling something which nobody understood, and then galloping on again.

" Some goddam drunk," said one of the Medfordites, and they all went back to bed.

I wasn't going to be cheated out of my order now, no matter what happened, and I don't think that Mr. Revere could have been drunk, because while he was with us at " The Bell in Hand," he had only four short ales. He had a lot of cheese, though.

Something seemed to have been the matter with him, however, because in every town that I rode through I found people just going back to bed after having been aroused up out of their sleep by a mysterious rider. I didn't tell them that it was Mr. Revere, or that it was probably some stunt to do with the shindig that he and Mr. Dawes were putting on for the North Church. I figured out that it was a little publicity stunt.

Finally, just as I got into Lexington, I saw my man getting off his horse at a house right alongside the Green. I rushed up and caught him just as he was going in. I introduced myself and told him that I represented the Juno Acid Bath Corporation of New York and asked him if he could give me a few minutes, as I had been following him all the way from Charlestown and had been to his office three days in succession. He said that he was busy right at that minute, but that if I wanted to come along with him upstairs he would talk business on the way. He asked me if I wasn't the man he had been talking to at " The Bell in Hand " and I said yes, and asked him how Podunk was. This got him in good humour and he said that we might as well sit right down then and that he would get someone else to do what he had to do. So he called a man-servant and told him to go right upstairs, wake up Mr. Hancock and Mr. Adams and tell them to get up, and no fooling. " Keep after them, Sambo," he said, " and don't let them roll over and go to sleep again. It's very important."

So we sat down in the living room and I got out our statement of sales for 1774 and showed him that, in face of increased competition, Juno had practically doubled its output. " There must be some reason for an acid outselling its competitors three to one," I said, " and that reason, Mr. Revere, is that a Juno product is a guaranteed product." He asked me about the extra sixpence a tin and I asked him if he would rather pay a sixpence less and get an inferior grade of acid and he said, " No." So I finally landed an order of three dozen tins of Vulcan No. 2 and a dozen jars of Acme Silver Polish, as Mr. Revere is a silversmith, also, on the side.

Took a look around Lexington before I went back to Boston, but didn't see any engraving plants. Lexington is pretty quiet right now.

Respectfully submitted,

THADDEUS OLIN.

Attached.

Expense Voucher

Juno Acid Bath Corp., New York

Thaddeus Olin, Agent.

Hotel in Boston		15s.
Stage fare		30s.
Meals (4 days)		28s.
Entertaining prospects	£3	4s.
Horse rent—Charlestown to Lexington and return ...	£2	6s.
Total Expense	£9	3s.
To Profit on three dozen tins of Vulcan No. 2		18s.
and One dozen jars Acme Silver Polish		4s.
	£1	2s.
Net Loss	£8	1s.

The Stranger within our Gates

ONE of the problems of child education which is not generally included in books on the subject is the Visiting Schoolmate. By this is meant the little friend whom your child brings home for the holidays. What is to be done with him, the Law reading as it does?

He is usually brought home because his own home is in Nevada, and if he went 'way out there for Christmas he would no sooner get there than he would have to turn right around and come back— an ideal arrangement on the face of it. But there is something in the idea of the child away from home at Christmas time that tears at the heart strings, and little George is received into the bosom of your family with open arms and a slight catch in the throat. Poor little nipper! He must call up his parents by telephone on Christmas Day; they will miss him so. (It later turns out that even when George's parents lived in Philadelphia he spent his vacations with friends, his parents being no fools.)

The presents turn out to be things he already has, only his are better.

For the first day George is a model of politeness. "George is a nice boy," you say to your son; "I wish you knew more like him." "George seems to be a very manly little chap for fourteen," your wife says after the boys have gone to bed. "I hope that Bill is impressed." Bill, as a matter of fact, does seem to have caught some of little George's gentility and reserve, and the hope for his future which had been practically abandoned is revived again under his schoolmate's influence.

The first indication that George's stay is not going to be a blessing comes at the table, when, with confidence born of one day's association, he announces flatly that he does not eat potatoes, lamb or peas, the main course of the meal consisting of potatoes, lamb and peas.

"Perhaps you would like an egg, George?" you suggest. "I hate eggs," says George, looking out the window while he waits for you to hit on something that he does like.

"I'm afraid you aren't going to get much to eat to-night, then, George," you say. "What is there for dessert?"

"A nice bread pudding with raisins," says your wife.

George, at the mention of bread pudding, gives what is knows as "the bird," a revolting sound made with the tongue and lower lip. "I can't eat raisins anyway," he adds, to be polite. "They make me come out in a rash."

"Ah-h! The old raisin-rash," you say. "Well, we'll keep you away from raisins, I guess. And just what is it that you can eat, George? You can tell me. I am your friend."

Under cross-examination it turns out that George can eat beets if they are cooked just right, a rare species of eggplant grown only in Nevada, and all the ice cream in the world. He will also cram down a bit of cake now and then for manners' sake.

All this would not be so bad if it were not for the fact that, coincidentally with refusing the lamb, George criticises your carving of it. "My father carves lamb across the grain instead of the way you do," he says, a little crossly.

"Very interesting," is your comment.

"My father says that only old ladies carve straight down like that," he goes on.

"Well, well," you say pleasantly between your teeth, "That makes me out sort of an old lady, doesn't it?"

"Perhaps you have a different kind of lamb in Nevada," you suggest, hacking off a large chunk. (You have never carved so badly.) "A kind that feeds on your special kind of eggplant."

"We don't have lamb very often," says George. "Mostly squab and duck."

"You stick to squab and duck, George," you say, "and it will be just dandy for that rash of yours. Here take this and like it!" And you toss him a piece of lamb which, oddly enough, is later found to have disappeared from his plate.

It also turns out later that George's father can build sailboats, make a monoplane that will really fly, repair a broken buzzer and imitate birds, none of which you can do and none of which you have ever tried to do, having given it to be understood that they *couldn't* be done. You begin to hate George's father almost as much as you do George.

"I suppose your father writes articles for the magazines, too, doesn't he, George?" you ask sarcastically.

"Sure," says George with disdain. "He does that Sundays—Sunday afternoons."

"Yes, sir," says George.

This just about cleans up George so far as you are concerned, but there are still ten more days of vacation. And during these ten days your son Bill is induced by George to experiment with electricity to the extent of blowing out all the fuses in the house and burning the cigarette lighter out of the sedan; he is also inspired to call the cook a German spy who broils babies, to insult several of the neighbours' little girls to the point of tears and reprisals, and to refuse spinach. You know that Bill didn't think of these things himself, as he never could have had the imagination.

On Christmas Day all the little presents that you got for George turn out to be things that he already has, only his are better. He incites Bill to revolt over the question of where the tracks to the electric train are to be placed (George maintaining that in his home they run through his father's bathroom, which is the only sensible place for tracks to run). He breaks several of little Barbara's more fragile presents and says that she broke them herself by not knowing how to work them. And the day ends with George running a high temperature and coming down with mumps, necessitating a quarantine and enforced residence in your house for a month.

This is just a brief summary of the Visiting Schoolmate problem. Granted that every child should have a home to go to at Christmas, could there not be some sort of state subsidy designed to bring their own homes on to such children as are unable to go home themselves? On such a day each home should be a sanctuary, where only members of the tribe can gather and overeat and quarrel. Outsiders just complicate matters, especially when outsiders cannot be spanked.

Evolution Sidelights

Showing Nature's Way of Taking Care of Her Young

ONE of the most fascinating chapters in the story of Evolution is that in which we see animals of a certain type change, through the ages, into animals of quite a different type, through a process of the survival of the fittest and adaptation to environment. These are pretty big words, I am afraid, but before we are through you will see what they mean, or you will take a sock on the nose.

Thus we learn that our present-day sheep, from whose warm blanket our silk socks are made, was once, in the early, early days of the earth, a member of the hermit-crab family. It was during the Palæozoic Age, before the great glaciers had swept down over the land leaving their trail of empty tins and old shoes, even before the waters had receded from the earth. So you can see how long ago it was! Just years and years.

Well, anyway, the hermit-crab of the Palæozoic Era lived in the slime and sulked. He didn't like being a hermit-crab. He didn't see any future in it. And, as the sun beat down on the earth, and the waters gradually receded, the crab was left high and dry on the beach and little Palæozoic children built forts on him. This got him pretty sore.

Now as the centuries went by and the sun continued to beat down on the earth, the color of the mud changed from reddish brown to a dirty grey. Formerly, the crabs who were reddish brown had been more or less hidden in the reddish brown mud, but now they stood out like a rainy Thursday, and it was the dirty grey crabs who were protected from the onslaughts of the hordes of crab devouring mantes which came down from the mountains. Gradually the red crabs became extinct, and the grey crabs, through their protective colouring, survived. The red crabs that you see to-day are a new batch, and anyway, don't ask questions.

The next step was ages and ages later, when the crab, in order to get food, began to stretch himself out to get to the grass which grew up along the edge of the beach. He also wanted to take a crack at this running business he had heard so much about. So, in another hundred million years, or, at any rate, a good long time, these crabs had developed teeth with which to pull up grass and chew it, and four legs on which to run. By this time it was late in April.

We finally see these four-legged herbivorous crabs who had managed to survive the rigours of the seasons, running, as sheep will, farther and farther north, where the weather grew colder and colder. This made it necessary for them to develop some protective covering, and those lucky crabs who were able to work themselves up into a sort of wool were the ones who stood the climate. The others froze to death and became soldiers' monuments.

And that is how Nature took care of the hermit-crab and turned him into a sheep.

The same thing happens right under our very eyes to-day, only quicker. Nature has endowed certain animals with the power to change colour at a second's notice, and thus elude pursuers. Of course, a simpler way for such animals would be to stay in the house all the time and make faces out the window at their enemies, but some of them, like the horse, simply have to go out-of-doors occasionally on business, and it is then that their ability to change colouring comes in so handy.

Having taken the horse as an example, we may as well continue. Professor Rossing, in his book, " Animal, Vegetable or Mineral ? " reports a case of a man who was chasing a bay mare to try to make her eat her breakfast. He had chased her all around the yard, both of them laughing so hard they could scarcely run. Suddenly, the mare, deciding that there had been enough of this foolishness, drew up alongside a red brick silo, and ducking her head slightly, changed colouring in an instant, taking on exactly the shade and markings of the brick surface. Her pursuer was dumbfounded, thinking that the mare had disappeared into thin air. As he drew near to the silo, to examine what he felt sure must be a trap door in the side, the mare romped away again, startling him so that he dropped the feed bag, and the chase was over. The mare, with Nature's aid, had won. How many of us can say the same ?

Fascinating Crimes

The Strange Case of the Vermont Judiciary

RESIDENTS of Water Street, Bellows Falls (Vt.), are not naturally sound sleepers, owing to the proximity of the Bellows Falls Light and Power Co. and its attendant thumpings, but fifteen years before the erection of the light-and-power plant there was nothing to disturb the slumbers of Water Streetites, with the possible exception of the bestial activities of Roscoe Erkle. For it was Mr. Erkle's whim to creep up upon people as they slept and, leaping on their chests, to cram poisoned biscuits into their mouths until they died, either from the poison or from choking on the crumbs.

A tolerant citizenry stood this as long as it could decently be expected to, and then had Roscoe Erkle arrested. It is not this phase of his career in which we are interested, however, so much as the remarkable series of events which followed.

His trial began at St. Albans, Franklin County, on Wednesday morning, May 7, 1881. Defending Erkle was an attorney appointed by the Court, Enos J. Wheefer. Mr. Wheefer, being deaf, had not heard the name of his client or he would never have taken the case. He thought for several days that he was defending Roscoe Conkling and had drawn up his case with Conkling in mind.

Atty. Herbert J. McNell represented the State and, as it later turned out, a tragic fate gave the case into the hands of Judge Alonso Presty for hearing.

Judge Presty was one of the leaders of the Vermont bar at the time and a man of impeccable habits. It was recalled after his untimely death that he had been something of a rounder in his day, having been a leader in barn-dancing circles while in law school, but since donning the sock and buskin his conduct had been propriety itself. Which make the events that we are about to relate all the more puzzling.

On the opening day of the trial, Atty. McNell was submitting as evidence passages from the prisoner's diary which indicated that the murders were not only premeditated but a source of considerable delight to Mr. Erkle. It might perhaps be interesting to give a sample page from the diary :

" *Oct.* 7—Cool and fair. Sharp tinge of Fall in the air. New shipment of arsenic arrived from W. Spent all day powdering biscuits and then toasting them. Look good enough to eat.

" *Oct.* 8—Raw, with N.E. wind. Betsy came in for a minute and we did anagrams. (EDITOR'S NOTE : *Betsy was Erkle's cow.*)

" *Oct.* 9—Still raw. Cleaned up Water Street on the left-hand side, with the exception of old Wassner who just wouldn't open his mouth. Home and read till after midnight. That man Carlyle certainly had the dope on the French Revolution, all right, all right."

As Atty. McNell read these excerpts from the diary in a droning voice, the breath of Vermont May-time wafted in at the open windows of the courtroom. Now and then a bee hummed in and out, as if to say: "Buz-z-z-z-z-z-z!" Judge Presty sat high above the throng, head resting on his hand, to all intents and purposes asleep.

Suddenly the attorney for the defendant arose and said: "I protest, Your Honour. I cannot hear what my learned colleague is saying, but I don't like his expression!"

There was silence while all eyes turned on the Judge. But the Judge did not move. Thinking that he had fallen asleep, as was his custom during the May term, the attorneys went on. It was not until he had gradually slipped forward into the glass of water which stood before him on his desk that it was discovered that he was dead!

The trial was immediately halted and an investigation begun. Nothing could be discovered about the Judge's person which would give a clue to his mysterious lapse except a tiny red spot just behind his right ear. This, however, was laid to indigestion and the Judge was buried.

Another trial was called for October 10, again in St. Albans. This time Judge Walter M. Bondy was presiding, and the same two attorneys opposed each other. Roscoe Erkle had, during the summer, raised a red beard and looked charming.

On the second day of the trial, while Atty. McNell was reading the prisoner's diary, Judge Bondy passed away quietly at his bench, with the same little red spot behind his right ear that had characterised the cadaver of his predecessor. The trial was again halted, and a new one set for the following May.

By this time, the matter had become one for serious concern. Erkle was questioned, but his only reply was: "Let them mind their own business, then." He had now begun to put pomade on his beard and had it parted in the middle, and, as a result, had married one of the richest spinsters in that section of Vermont.

We need not go into the repetitious account of the succeeding trials. Suffice it to say that the following May Judge Rapf died at his post, the following October Judge Orsenigal, the May following that a Judge O'Heel, who had been imported from New Hampshire without being told the history of the case, and the succeeding solstices saw the mysterious deaths of Judges Wheefer (the counsel for the defence in the first trial, who had, in the meantime, been appointed Judge because of his deafness), Rossberg, Wheland, Rock and Brady. And, in each case, the little telltale mark behind the ear.

The State then decided to rest its case and declare it *nol-prossed*. Judges were not so plentiful in Vermont that they could afford to go on at this rate. Erkle was released on his own recognisance, took up the study of law, and is, at latest accounts, a well-to-do patent attorney in Oldham. Every May and every October he reports at St. Albans to see if they want to try him again, but the Court laughingly postpones the case until the next term, holding its hand over its right ear the while.

The Four-in-Hand Outrage

WHAT has happened to four-in-hand ties that they refuse to slide around under the collar any more? Or am I just suffering from a persecution complex?

For maybe ten years I have been devoted to the soft collar or sport model, the polo shirt, and other informal modes in collarings affected by the *jeunesse dorée*. They have not been particularly adapted to playing up my good points in personal appearance, but they are easy to slip into in the morning.

*have been devoted to informal modes of Collarings affected
by the* jeunesse dorée.

With the approach of portly middle-age, however, and the gradual but relentless assumption of power in the financial world, it seemed to me that I ought to dress the part. When a man goes into a bank to ask to have his note extended he should at least wear a stiff collar and a four-in-hand of some rich, dark material, preferably a foulard. He owes it to himself.

The tie refuses to budge.

So I laid in a stock of shirts (two) which called for either stiff collars or a knotted bandana, and then set about digging up some collars to go with them. My old stock of " Greywoods 14½ " which I used to wear in high-school proved useless. They were of the mode, so flashy in those days, which came close together in front, allowing just a tip of the knitted club-tie to peek out from under the corners. And, owing to a temporary increase in neck-size (I can reduce it at any time by dieting for two or three days), 14½ is no longer my number. So I bought several styles of a more modern collar and prepared to throw the world of fashion into a tumult by appearing in formal neckwear on, let us say, the following Wednesday at high noon.

But in the ten years which have elapsed since I last tied a four-in-hand under a stiff collar something perverse has been injected into the manufacture of either the ties or the collars. My male readers will recognise a manœuvre which I can best designate as the Final Tug, the last short pull-around of the tie under the collar before tightening the knot. This, under the present system, has become practically impossible. The tie refuses to budge; I pull and yank, take the collar off and re-arrange the tie, try gentle tactics, followed suddenly by a deceptive upward jerk, but this gets me nothing. The knot stays loosely off-centre and the tie appears to be stuck somewhere underneath the collar at a point perhaps three inches to the right. After two minutes of this mad wrenching one of three things happens—the tie rips, the collar tears, or I strangle to death in a horrid manner with eyes bulging and temples distended, a ghastly caricature of my real self.

Now this is a very strange thing to have happened in ten years. It can't be that I have forgotten how. It can't be that I have lost that amount of strength through loose living. It must be that some deliberate process has been adopted by the manufacturers to prevent four-in-hands from slipping under collars. What their idea can be is a mystery. You'd think they would *want* to make things as easy for their patrons as possible. But no! Modern business *efficiency*, I suppose! The manufacturers were *in conference*, I suppose! Rest-rooms for their women employees . . . oh, yes! Time clocks, charts, paper drinking cups . . . òh, yes! But collars that hold ties immovable, and ties that stick in collars. That's what *we* get. That's what the Public gets. Prohibition was foisted on our boys while they were overseas, and while I was wearing soft collars the Powers-That-Be were putting the devil into stiff ones, so that when I come back to wearing them again I strangle myself to death. A fine civilisation, I must say!

Trout Fishing

I NEVER knew very much about trout fishing anyway, and I certainly had no inkling that a trout fisher had to be so deceitful until I read " Trout Fishing in Brooks," by G. Garrow-Green. The thing is appalling. Evidently the sport is nothing but a constant series of compromises with one's better nature, what with sneaking about pretending to be something that one is not, trying to fool the fish into thinking one thing when just the reverse is true, and in general behaving in an underhanded and tricky manner throughout the day.

The very first and evidently the most important exhortation in the book is, " Whatever you do, keep out of sight of the fish." Is that open and above board? Is it honorable?

F

" Trout invariably lie in running water with their noses pointed against the current, and therefore whatever general chance of concealment there may be rests in fishing from behind them. The moral is that the brook angler must both walk and fish upstream."

It seems as if a lot of trouble might be saved the fisherman, in case he really didn't want to walk upstream but had to get to some point downstream before 6 o'clock, to adopt some disguise which would deceive the fish into thinking that he had no intention of catching them anyway. A pair of blue glasses and a cane would give the effect of the wearer being blind and harmless, and could be thrown aside very quickly when the time came to show one's self in one's true colours to the fish. If there were two anglers they might talk in loud tones about their dislike for fish in any form, and then, when the trout were quite reassured and swimming close to the bank they could suddenly be shot with a pistol.

But a little further on comes a suggestion for a much more elaborate bit of subterfuge.

The author says that in the early season trout are often engaged with larvæ at the bottom and do not show on the surface. It is then a good plan, he says, to sink the flies well, moving in short jerks to imitate nymphs.

You can see that imitating a nymph will call for a lot of rehearsing, but I doubt very much if moving in short jerks is the way in which to go about it. I have never actually seen a nymph, though if I had I should not be likely to admit it, and I can think of no possible way in which I could give an adequate illusion of being one myself. Even the most stupid of trout could easily divine that I was masquerading, and then the question would immediately arise in his mind : " If he is not a nymph, then what is his object in going about like that trying to imitate one ? He is up to no good, I'll be bound."

And crash ! away would go the trout before I could put my clothes back on.

There is an interesting note on the care and feeding of worms on page 67. One hundred and fifty worms are placed in a tin and allowed to work their way down into packed moss.

" A little fresh milk poured in occasionally is sufficient food," writes Mr. Garrow-Green, in the style of Dr. Holt. " So disposed, the worms soon become bright, lively and tough."

It is easy to understand why one should want to have bright worms, so long as they don't know that they are bright and try to show off before company, but why deliberately set out to make them tough ? Good manners they may not be expected to acquire, but a worm with a cultivated vulgarity sounds intolerable. Imagine 150 very tough worms all crowded together in one tin ! " Canaille " is the only word to describe it.

I suppose that it is my ignorance of fishing parlance which makes the following sentence a bit hazy :

" Much has been written about bringing a fish downstream to help drown it, as no doubt it does ; still, this is often impracticable."

I can think of nothing more impracticable than trying to drown a fish under any conditions, upstream or down, but I suppose that Mr. Garrow-Green knows what he is talking about.

And in at least one of his passages I follow him perfectly. In speaking of the time of day for fly fishing in the spring he says :

" ' Carpe diem ' is a good watchword when trout are in the humour." At least, I know a good pun when I see one.

"*Ask that Man*"

THIS is written for those men who have wives who are constantly insisting on their asking questions of officials.

For years I was troubled with the following complaint : Just as soon as we started out on a trip of any kind, even if it were only to the corner of the street, Doris began forcing me to ask questions of people. If we weren't quite sure of the way : " Why don't you ask that man ? He could tell you." If there was any doubt as to the best place to go to get chocolate ice cream, she would say : " Why don't you ask that boy in uniform ? He would be likely to know."

I can't quite define my aversion to asking questions of strangers.

My voice isn't very reliable in crises.

From snatches of family battles which I have heard drifting up from railway stations and street corners, I gather that there are a great many men who share my dislike for it, as well as an equal number of women who, like Doris, believe it to be the solution of most of this world's problems. The man's dread is probably that of making himself appear a pest or ridiculously uninformed. The woman's insistence is based probably on experience which has taught her that *any* one, no matter who, knows more about things in general than her husband.

Furthermore, I never know exactly how to begin a request for information. If I preface it with, " I beg your pardon ! " the stranger is likely not to hear, especially if he happens to be facing in another

I gather that there are a great many men who share my dislike for it.

direction, for my voice isn't very reliable in crises and sometimes makes no intelligible sound at all until I have been talking for fully a minute. Often I say, " I beg your pardon ! " and he turns quickly and says, " What did you say ? " Then I have to repeat, " I beg your pardon ! " and he asks, quite naturally, " What for ? " Then I am stuck. Here I am, begging a perfect stranger's pardon, and for no apparent reason under the sun. The wonder is that I am not knocked down oftener.

It was to avoid going through life under this pressure that I evolved the little scheme detailed herewith. It cost me several thousand dollars, but Doris is through with asking questions of outsiders.

We had started on a little trip to Boston. I could have found out where the Boston train was in a few minutes had I been left to myself. But Doris never relies on the signs. Someone must be asked, too, just to make sure. Confronted once by a buck-board literally swathed in banners which screamed in red letters, " This bus goes to the State Fair Grounds," I had to go up to the driver (who had on his cap a flag reading " To the State Fair Grounds ") and ask him if this bus surely went to the State Fair Grounds. He didn't even answer me.

So when Doris said : " Go and ask that man where the Boston train leaves from," I gritted my teeth and decided that the time had come. Simulating conversation with him, I really asked him nothing, and returned to Doris, saying, " Come on. He says it goes from Track 10."

Eight months later we returned home. The train that left Track 10 was the Chicago Limited, which I had taken deliberately. In Chicago I again falsified what " the man " told me, and instead of getting on the train back to New York we went to Little Rock, Arkansas. Every time I had to ask where the best hotel was, I made up information which brought us out into the suburbs, cold and hungry. Many nights we spent wandering through the fields looking for some place that never existed, or else in the worst hotel in town acting on what I said was the advice of " that kind-looking man in uniform."

From Arkansas, we went into Mexico, and once, guided by what I told her had been the directions given me by the man at the news-stand in Vera Cruz, we made a sally into the swamps of Central America, in whatever that first republic is on the way south. After that, Doris began to lose faith in what strange men could tell us. One day, at a little station in Mavicos, I said : " Wait a minute, till I ask that man what is the best way to get back into America," and she said, sobbing : " Don't ask anybody. Just do what you think is best." Then I knew that the fight was over. In ten days I had her limp form back in New York and from that day to this she hasn't once suggested that I ask questions of a stranger.

The funny part of it is, I constantly find myself asking them. I guess the humiliation came in being told to ask.

Cell-formations and
Their Work

IT is only recently that science has found out the exact structure of the tiny cell formations which go to make up life. Only yesterday, in fact.

Every higher animal starts life as a single cell. This much is obvious. Look at the rainbow. Look at the formation of frost on the window pane. Don't look now. Wait a minute. . . . Now look.

This cell measures no more than 1/125 of an inch in diameter at first, but you mustn't be discouraged. It looks like nothing at all, even under the strongest microscope, and, before we knew just how important they were, they were often thrown away. We now know that if it were not for these tiny, tiny cells, we should none of us be here to-day. This may or may not be a recommendation for the cells. *Quien sabe* ?

Shortly after the cell decides to go ahead with the thing, it gets lonely and divides itself up into three similar cells, just for company's sake and to have someone to talk to. They soon find out that they aren't particularly congenial, so they keep on dividing themselves up into other cells until there is a regular mob of them. Then they elect an entertainment committee and give a show.

After the show, there is a fight, and the thing breaks up into different cliques or groups. One group think they are white corpuscles or *phagocytes*. Others go around saying that they are *red* corpuscles and to hell with the white.

The other groups of cells devote themselves to music, aesthetic dancing, and the formation of starch which goes into dress shirts. They are all very happy and very busy, and it's nobody's business *what* they do when they aren't working. We certainly are not going to snoop into that here.

We must take up, however, the work of the brain cells, as it is in the brain that the average man of to-day does his thinking. (Aha-ha-ha-ha-ha-ha !)

Oh, let's *not* take up the brain cells. You know as much about them as anybody does, and what's the use anyway ? Suppose you *do* learn something to-day. You're likely to die to-morrow, and there you are.

And we *must* go into the question of the size of these cells. That really is important. In about 1/150000 of a cubic inch of blood there are some five million cells afloat. This is, as you will see, about the population of the City of London, except that the cells don't wear any hats. Thus, in our whole body, there are perhaps (six times seven is forty-two, five times eight is forty, put down nought

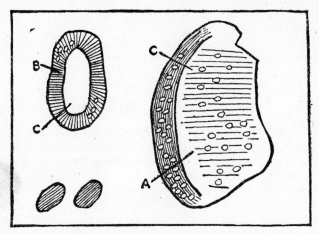

Differentiation of cells in the lens of an eye.
Doesn't mean a thing.

and carry your four, eight times nine is seventy-two and four is seventy-six, put down six and carry your seven and then, adding, six, four, three, one, six, nought, nought, nought), oh, about a billion or so of these red corpuscles alone, not counting overhead and breakage. In the course of time, that runs into figures.

Now when it comes to reproduction, you have to look out. In the cuttlefish, for example, there is what is known as " greesion " or budding. The organism as a whole remains unaltered, except that one small portion of it breaks off and goes into business for itself. This, of course, makes a very pretty picture, but gets nowhere. In the case of multicellular animals, like the orange, it results in a frightful confusion.

We should have said that there are two classes of animals, unicellular and multicellular. From the unicellular group we get our coal, iron, wheat and ice, and from the multicellular our salt, pepper, chutney and that beautiful silk dress which milady wears so proudly. Woollen and leather goods we import.

You will see then that by grafting a piece of one species on another species, you can mix the cells and have all kinds of fun. Winkler, in 1902, grafted a piece of Solanum (the genus to which the potato belongs) on to a stock of another kind, and then, after the union had been established, cut the stem across, just at the point of junction. The bud was formed of the intermingled tissues of the two species and was most peculiar looking.

Winkler was arrested.

A Talk
to Young Men

Graduation Address on " The Decline of Sex "

TO you, young men who only recently were graduated from our various institutions of learning (laughter), I would bring a message, a message of warning and yet, at the same time, a message of good cheer. Having been out in the world a whole month, it is high time that you learned something about the Facts of Life, something about how wonderfully Nature takes care of the thousand and one things which go to make up what some people jokingly call our " sex " life. I hardly know how to begin. Perhaps " Dear Harry " would be as good a way as any.

You all have doubtless seen, during your walks in the country, how the butterflies and bees carry pollen from one flower to another ? It is very dull and you should be very glad that you are not a bee or a butterfly, for where the fun comes in *that* I can't see. However, they think that they are having a good time, which is all that is necessary, I suppose. Some day a bee is going to get hold of a real book on the subject, and from then on there will be mighty little pollen-toting done or I don't know my bees.

Well, anyway, if you have noticed carefully how the bees carry pollen from one flower to another (and there is no reason why you should have noticed carefully as there is nothing to see), you will have wondered what connection there is between this process and that of animal reproduction. I may as well tell you right now that there is no connection at all, and so your whole morning of bee-stalking has been wasted.

We now come to the animal world. Or rather, first we come to One Hundred and Twenty-fifth Street, but you don't get off there. The animal world is next, and off you get. And what a sight meets your eyes ! My, my ! It just seems as if the whole world were topsy-turvy.

The next time you are at your grocer's buying gin, take a look at his eggs. They really are some hen's eggs, but they belong to the grocer now, as he has bought them and is entitled to sell them. So they really *are* his eggs, funny as it may sound to anyone who doesn't know. If you will look at these eggs, you will see that each one is *almost* round, but not *quite*. They are more of an " egg shape." This may strike you as odd at first, until you learn that this is Nature's way of distinguishing eggs from large golf balls. You see, Mother Nature takes no chances. She used to, but she learned her lesson. And that is a lesson that all of you must learn as well. It is called Old Mother Nature's Lesson, and begins on page 145.

Now, these eggs have not always been like this. That stands to reason. They once had something to do with a hen or they wouldn't be called hen's eggs. If they are called duck's eggs, that means that they had something to do with a duck. Who can tell me what it means if they are called " ostrich's eggs " ? . . . That's right.

But the egg is not the only thing that had something to do with a hen. Who knows what else there was ? . . . That's right.

Now the rooster is an entirely different sort of bird from the hen. It is very proud and has a red crest on the top of his head. This red crest is put there by Nature so that the hen can see the rooster coming in a crowd and can hop into a taxi or make a previous engagement if she wants to. A favourite dodge of a lot of hens when they see the red crest of the rooster making in their direction across the barnyard is to work up a sick headache. One of the happiest and most contented roosters I ever saw was one who had had his red crest chewed off in a fight with a dog. He also wore sneakers.

But before we take up this phase of the question (for it is a question), let us go back to the fish kingdom. Fish are probably the worst example that you can find ; in the first place, because they work under water, and in the second, because they don't know anything· You won't find one fish in a million that has enough sense to come in when it rains. They are just stupid, that's all, and nowhere is their stupidity more evident than in their sex life.

Take, for example, the carp. The carp is one of the least promising of all the fish. He has practically no forehead and brings nothing at all to a conversation. Now the mother carp is swimming around some fine spring day when suddenly she decides that it would be nice to have some children. So she makes out a deposit slip and deposits a couple million eggs on a rock (all this goes on *under* water, mind you, of all places). This done, she adjusts her hat, powders her nose, and swims away, a woman with a past.

It is not until all this is over and done with that papa enters the picture, and then only in an official capacity. Papa's job is very casual. He swims over the couple of million eggs and takes a chance that by sheer force of personality he can induce half a dozen of them to hatch out. The remainder either go to waste or are blacked up to represent caviar.

So you will see that the sex life of a fish is nothing much to brag about. It never would present a problem in a fish community as it does in ours. No committees ever have to be formed to regulate it, and about the only way in which a fish can go wrong is through drink or stealing. This makes a fish's life highly unattractive, you will agree, for, after a time, one would get very tired of drinking and stealing.

We have now covered the various agencies of Nature for populating the earth with the lesser forms of life. We have purposely omitted any reference to the reproduction of those unicellular organisms which reproduce by dividing themselves up into two, four, eight, etc., parts without any outside assistance at all. This method is too silly even to discuss.

We now come to colours. You all know that if you mix yellow with blue you get green. You also get green if you mix cherries and milk. (Just kidding. Don't pay any attention.) The derivation of one colour from the mixture of two other colours is not generally considered a sexual phenomenon, but that is because the psycho-analysts haven't got around to it yet. By next season it won't be safe to admit that you like to paint, or you will be giving yourself away as an inhibited old uncle-lover and debauchee. The only thing that the sex-psychologists can't read a sexual significance into is trap shooting, and they are working on that now.

All of which brings us to the point of wondering if it *all* isn't a gigantic hoax. If the specialists fall down on trap shooting, they are going to begin to doubt the whole structure which they have erected, and before long there is going to be a reaction which will take the form of an absolute negation of sex. An Austrian scientist has already come out with the announcement that there is no such thing as a hundred per cent. male or a hundred per cent. female. If this is true, it is really a big step forward. It is going to throw a lot of people out of work, but think of the money that will be saved!

And so, young men, my message to you is this : Think the thing over carefully and examine the evidence with fair-minded detachment. And if you decide that, within the next ten years, sex is going out of style, make your plans accordingly. Why not be pioneers in the new movement ?

The Homelike Hotel

ONE of the chief factors in the impending crash of the American Home as an institution is the present craze for making so many other places " home-like." We have homelike hotels, home-like barber shops, homelike auditoriums, and, so they tell me, home-like jails. A man can't go into a shop to get his skates sharpened without being made to feel that, if he has any appreciation for atmosphere at all, he ought really to send for his trunks and settle down and live right there in the skate sharpening place. It is getting so that a home loving man doesn't know which way to turn.

The hotels were the leaders in this campaign to make the home seem unhomelike by comparison. There was a time when a hotel was simply a place in which you slept ; that is, if you were a good sleeper. You went in and registered and the man who pushed the book out at you turned his collar around and became the boy who took your bag up (possibly in one of those new-fangled lifts which you were sure would never replace the horse—at least, not in your affections).

The room, as you entered it, seemed to be a species of closet, smelling strongly of straw matting and rug threads, and, after a good look at the cherry bureau and its duplicating mirror and a tug at the rope which was coiled by the window in case you wanted to lasso anyone, you turned out the hanging bulb over the bed (making a barely perceptible difference in the lighting of the room), and went out into the street to find a place to sit until bedtime. You would no more have thought of sitting in your room than you would have thought of getting into one of the bureau drawers and lolling around with a good book.

The first sign that the hotels were going in for the homey stuff in a big way was when they began hanging pictures on the walls. Either they didn't get the right pictures or they weren't hung properly. At any rate, the first hotel wall pictures were not successful in giving a homelike atmosphere. There were usually pastels showing two ladies with a fan, or two fans and one lady, with a man in knee breeches hovering about in the background. The girl with the broken jug was also a great favourite in the early days of hotel decoration. She still is doing very well, as a matter of fact, and you will find her in even the most up-to-date hostelries, giving what is hoped will be a final touch of bonhomie to the room. Well, she doesn't, and the sooner hotel managements are brought to realise it, the better it will be for them.

In fact, the whole problem of what pictures to hang on the walls of a hotel room is still in a state of flux. Until they get away from those little French garden scenes, with fans and sun dials as the chief props, they are never going to make me feel at home. And they do not help matters any by introducing etchings showing three boats lying alongside a dock or 17 geese flying South. It seems to me that the picture-hangers in hotels are striving too hard for good taste. What we want is not good taste in our hotel pictures, but something to look at. If you are going to live in the room with a picture all the rest of your life, good taste is all right. But for overnight give me something a little daring, with a lot of red in it.

There is another development in the equipment of hotel rooms which, while it does not exactly make the quarters attractive, keeps the guest interested while he is in the room. I refer to the quantity of reading matter which is placed at his disposal. This does not mean the little magazines that some hotels place by the bedside, in the hope that you will sit up so late reading that you will have to send down for a glass of milk and some crackers at midnight. I don't think people read those as much as they are supposed to. I don't think they even look at the pictures as much as they are supposed to.

But there is a trait which is almost universal among hotel guests and which is being catered to more and more by the managements.

It is the tendency, amounting almost to a fascination, to read every word of every sign which is displayed around the room. You know very well that the chances are that not one sign out of ten will have any bearing on you or your life in that room. And yet, almost as soon as the bellboy has left, you amble around the room, reading little notices which have been slipped under the glass bureau top tacked to the door, or tucked in the mirror. Not only do you read them once, but you usually go over them a second time, hoping that, maybe there is something of interest which eluded you in the first reading.

I had occasion last week to share a hotel room with a man who was at Atlantic City with me on business. We were shown up by the boy, who went through all the regulation manœuvres of opening the window (which has to be shut immediately after he has gone), putting the bags on the stool (from which they have to be removed for unpacking), pushing open the door to the bathroom to show you where it is and to prevent your going into the next room by mistake, and making such financial adjustments as may be necessary. This completed, I reminded George that we were already late for our first appointment, and started for the door to go downstairs.

George, however, was busy at something over by the bureau. " Just a minute," he said, in a preoccupied tone. He was bending over the glass top as if he had found a deposit of something that might possibly turn out to be gold.

Impatiently I went over to grab him by the arm and pull him along. I saw he was reading a little notice, printed in red, which had been tucked under the glass. Determined to see what this fascinating message was that had riveted George to the spot, I read :

The use of alcohol lamps, sterno lamps, and all other flame-producing appliances, as well as electric devices, is positively forbidden.

" That makes it rather tough for you, doesn't it," I said, " with all your flame-producing appliances ? Shall we go to another hotel ? "

George said nothing, but went to get his hat. I sauntered over to the door to wait for him, but my eye was caught by a neatly printed sign which, although I knew that it would contain nothing which could possibly affect me personally, I was utterly unable to keep from reading :

In accepting garments for valet service it is thoroughly understood that they do not contain money, jewellery, or any other articles of value, and, consequently——

" Come on, come on ! " said George. " We're late now ! "

" Just a minute ! " It was I this time who had the preoccupied air. It was I whose eyes were glued to the tiny card and who could not leave until I had finished its stirring message——

—consequently the hotel's management or any of its staff will not be held responsible for the return of anything but the garments originally delivered.

" O.K. ! " I announced briskly. " Come on ! "

But George had found another sign on the wall by the door. This time we both read it together in silence.

Do not turn thumb latch when leaving room. Door is self-locking. Use thumb latch only when in room.

"What thumb latch is that?" George said, looking over the assortment of latches and catches on the door.

"This is it here," I said, equally engrossed.

"Don't turn it!" cried George, in terror. "It says not to turn it."

"Who's turning it?" I snapped back. "I was just seeing how it worked. Who would want to turn it, anyway?"

"You can't tell," replied George. "Somebody might have this room who had a terrible hunch for turning thumb latches. A hotel has to deal with a lot of strange eggs."

"What would happen if you did turn it?" I asked.

George shuddered. "It might transform the whole hotel into a pumpkin under our very feet," he said, in a low voice.

"Don't be so jumpy," I said, impatiently. "That sort of thing belongs to the Middle Ages—and, besides, it used to happen only at the stroke of midnight."

"What time is it now?" asked George. He was in a cold sweat.

"A quarter to five," I said, looking at my watch. "There's not much sense in going to that four-o'clock date now."

George agreed, so we took off our hats and spent the rest of the afternoon roaming about the room, reading signs to our hearts' content. We were rewarded by several even duller notices than the ones we had already studied and by a good 15 minutes over the 21 provisions of Act 146 of the state Legislature making it compulsory for the management of all inns, hotels, and boarding houses to maintain a safe in the office for the reception of valuables belonging to the guests.

"That's an old one," said George. "I've read that before."

"It's good, though," I said. "It always makes great reading. After all, old notices are best."

So we had dinner sent up to the room in order to complete our reading of the hotel laundry list (George flying into a rage at the charge of 75 cents for "dressing sacques") and, by bedtime, had cleaned up the entire supply of printed matter and were well into the Atlantic City telephone book.

If the hotels want to go still further in their campaigns to make their rooms interesting for their guests, I would suggest the introduction of a sort of treasure hunt for each room. On each door could be tacked a little legend saying something like: "I can be found by going (1) to the top of the possession of an old English queen, (2) under an article, beginning with 'W,' highly prized by astronomers, (3) between two Indian wigwam attachments, (4) underneath an American revolutionary firearm."

The guest could then spend his evenings trying to figure out these hiding places and perhaps emerge richer by a cigarette lighter or one of those face cloths done up in tissue paper envelopes which the hotels are so crazy to have you take away. It wouldn't be so much the value of the prize as the fun of finding it, and it would serve

We spent the rest of the afternoon reading signs to our hearts' content.

the purpose which seems to be the aim of all modern hostelries—
namely : to keep the guests out of the open air and to prevent them
from going home.

Sporting Life in America: Dozing

WE Americans are a hardy race, and hardy races need a lot of sleep. Sleep, that knits up the ravell'd sleave of care," Shakespeare has called it, and, except for the fact that it doesn't mean much, it is a pretty good simile. I often think of it myself just as I am dropping off into a light doze : Sleep, that sleeves up the raveled care of . . . knit, that sleeps up the shaveled neeve of pfor—pff—prpf—orpffff' (*trailing off into a low whistle*)."

One of the most charming manifestations of sleep which we, as a nation, indulge in as a pastime is the Doze. By the Doze I mean those little snatches of sleep which are caught now and then during the day, usually with the collar on and choking slightly, with the head inclined coyly to one side, during which there is a semiconscious attempt to appear as if we were really awake. It is in this department of sleep that we are really at our best.

Of course, there is one form of doze which, to the casual observer or tourist, gives the appearance of legitimate sleep. This is the short doze, or " quickie," which is taken just after the main awakening in the morning. The alarm rings, or the Lord High Chamberlain taps us on the shoulder (in the absence of a chamberlain a relative will do. And right here I would like to offer for examination that type of sadistic relative who takes actual delight in awakening people. They hover about with ghoulish anticipation until the minute arrives when they may legitimately begin their dirty work, and then, leering unpleasantly, they shake the sleeper roughly with a " Come, come ! Time to get up ! " and wait right there until he is actually out on the cold floor in his bare feet. There is something radically wrong with such people, and the sooner they are exposed as pathological cases the better it will be for the world). I'm sorry. I didn't mean to be nasty about it.

At any rate, we are awakened and look at the clock. There are five minutes before it is absolutely necessary to get out of bed. If we leave shaving until night, there might even be fifteen minutes. If we leave dressing until we get to the office, snatching our clothes from the chair and carrying them downtown on our arm, there might even be half an hour more for a good, health-giving nap. Who knows ? Perhaps those few minutes of extra sleep might make us just ten times as efficient during the day ! That is what we must think of—efficiency. We must sacrifice our petty opinions on the matter and think of the rest of the day and our efficiency. There is no doubt that fifteen minutes' more sleep would do wonders for us, no matter how little we really want to take it.

By the time we have finished this line of argument we are out pretty fairly cold again, but not so cold that we are not conscious of anyone entering the room. We feel that they are going to say : " Come, come, don't go back to sleep again ! " and we forestall this

warning with a brisk " I know ! I know ! I'm just thinking ! "
This is said with one eye partially open and one tiny corner of the
brain functioning.   The rest of our powers add up to a total loss.

It is one of Nature's wonders how a man can carry on an argument
with someone standing beside his bed and still be asleep to all intents
and purposes. Not a very good argument, perhaps, and one in
which many important words are missing or indistinct, but still an
argument. It is an argument, however, which seldom wins, the
state of justice in the world being what it is to-day.

Dozing before arising does not really come within the range of
this treatise. What we are concerned with are those little lapses
when we are fully dressed, when we fondly believe that no one notices.
Riding on a train, for example.

There is the short-distance doze in a day coach, probably the most
humiliating form of train sleeping. In this the elbow is rested on
the window sill and the head placed in the hand in an attitude of
thought. The glass feels very cool on the forehead and we rest
it there, more to cool off than anything else. The next thing we
know the forehead (carrying the entire head with it) has slid down
the length of the slippery pane and we have received a rather nasty
bang against the woodwork. They shouldn't keep their glass so
slippery. A person is likely to get badly hurt that way.

However, back again goes the forehead against the pane in its
original position, with the hand serving more or less as a buffer,
until another skid occurs, this time resulting in an angry determination
to give the whole thing up entirely and sit up straight in the seat.
Some dozers will take four or five slides without whimpering, going
back each time for more with apparently undiminished confidence
in their ability to see the thing through.

It is a game that you can't beat, however, and the sooner you sit
up straight in your seat, the sooner you will stop banging your head.

Dozing in a Pullman chair is not so dangerous, as one does not
have the risk of the sliding glass to cope with, but it is even less lovely
in its appearance.   Here the head is allowed to sink back against the
antimacassar—just for a minute to see if the headrest is really as
comfortable as it seems. It is then but the work of a minute for

the mouth to open slightly and the head to tip roguishly to the right, and there you are—as pretty a picture as one would care to see. You are very lucky if, when you come to and look about, you do not find your neighbours smiling indulgently at some little vagaries of breathing or eccentricities of facial expression which you have been permitting yourself.

The game in all this public dozing is to act, on awakening, as if you had known all along what you were doing. If your neighbours are smiling, you should smile back, as if to say : " Fooled you that time ! You thought I was asleep, didn't you ? "

If they are not quite so rude as to smile, but look quickly back at their reading on seeing your eyes open, you should assume a brisk, businesslike expression indicating that you have been thinking out some weighty business problem with your eyes closed, and, now that you have at last come on its solution, that it is snap-snap ! back to work for you ! If, after a furtive look around, you discover that no one has caught you at it, then it will do no harm to give it another try, this time until your collar chokes you into awakening with a strangling gasp.

The collar, however, is not always an impediment to public dozing. In the theatre, for example, a good, stiff dress collar and shirt bosom have been known to hold the sleeper in an upright position when otherwise he might have plunged forward and banged his head on the back of the seat in front.

In my professional capacity as play reviewer I had occasion to experiment in the various ways of sitting up straight and still snatching a few winks of health-giving sleep. I found that by far the safest is to keep one's heavy overcoat on, especially if it is made of some good, substantial material which will hold a sagging torso erect within its folds. With a good overcoat, reinforced by a stiff dress shirt and a high collar, one may even go beyond the dozing stage and sink into a deep, refreshing slumber, and still not be made conspicuous by continual lurchings and plungings. Of course, if you are an uneasy sleeper and given to thrashing about, you will find that even a heavy overcoat will let you down once in a while. But for the average man, who holds approximately the same position after he has gone to sleep, I don't think that this method can go wrong. Its only drawback is that you are likely to get a little warm along about the middle of the second act.

If you don't want to wear your overcoat in the theatre, the next best method is to fold the arms across the chest and brace the chin against the dress collar, exerting a slight upward pressure with the arms against the shirt front. This, however, can be used only for the lightest of dozes, as, once unconsciousness has set in .the pressure relaxes and over you go.

Dozing at a play, however refreshing, makes it a bit difficult to follow the argument on the stage, as occasionally the nap drags itself out into a couple of minutes and you awake to find a wholly fresh set of characters on the scene, or even a wholly fresh scene.

This is confusing. It is therefore wise to have someone along with you who will alternate watches with you, dozing when you are awake and keeping more or less alert while you are dozing. In this way you can keep abreast of what has been happening.

This, unfortunately, is impossible in personal conversations. If you slip off into a quick coma late some evening when your *vis-à-vis* is telling you about South America or a new solvent process, it is usually pretty difficult to pick up the thread where you dropped it. You may remember that the last words he was saying were " —which is situated at the mouth of the Amazon," but that isn't going to help you much if you come to just as he is asking you : " What would *you* say are ? " As in the personal-conversation doze the eyes very seldom completely close (it is more of a turning back of the eyeballs than a closing of the lids) you may escape detection if you have a ready answer for the emergency. I find that " Well, I don't know," said very slowly and deliberately, will fit almost any question that has been asked you. " Yes " and " No " should never be offered

as they might make you sound even sillier than you look. If you say : " Well, I—don't—know," it will give you a chance to collect your wits (what few there are left) and may lead your questioner into answering the thing himself.

At any rate, it will serve as a stall. If there are other people present, some one of them is quite likely to come to your rescue and say something which will tip you off as to the general subject under discussion. From then on, you will have to fight your own battle. I can't help you.

The whole problem is one which calls for a great deal of thought. If we can develop some way in which a man can doze and still keep from making a monkey of himself, we have removed one of the big obstacles to human happiness in modern civilisation. It goes without saying that we don't get enough sleep while we are in bed ; so we have got to get a little now and then while we are at work or at play. If we can find some way to keep the head up straight, the mouth closed, and just enough of the brain working to answer questions, we have got the thing solved right there.

I am working on it right now, as a matter of fact, but I find it a little difficult to keep awake.

The Mystery of
Bridge-Building

I AM not much of a one to be writing on bridge building, having never really built a bridge myself, but if the reader (you) will overlook a little vagueness in some of the directions, I myself will overlook the fact that the reader has no right to criticise, unless, of course, he happens to be a professional bridge builder himself.

It has always seemed to me that the most difficult part of building a bridge would be the start. What does a man do first when he sets out to build a bridge? Granted he has his plans all drawn up and enough food and drink to last him a month. He is standing on one bank of a river and wants to build a bridge across to the other bank. What is the first thing that he does? (I seem to be asking all the questions.)

I suppose that he takes a shovel and digs a little hole, and has his picture taken doing it. Maybe somebody waves a flag. I have seen photographs of such a ceremony, but they never show what happens next. Frankly, I would be up against it if any one were to put me on one bank of a river and say: " Build a bridge across to the other bank." I might be able to finish it if some one would start it for me, but as for making the first move I would be left blushing furiously.

I once heard of a man who was confronted by just this emergency. It had got around somehow that he was an authority on bridgework (as a matter of fact, he was a dentist), and when the people in a neighbouring town wanted a bridge built they sent for him. He was an easy-going sort of chap, and after they had given him a big dinner and a good cigar he didn't have the heart to tell them that he really knew nothing about the sort of bridge building that they wanted. He kept meaning to tell them, but they were so nice and evidently had so much confidence in him that he hated to spoil their good time, especially after he had eaten their dinner. So he just sat tight and let things take their course.

Pretty soon he found himself on the left bank of the river, with a brass band huddled around him and a lot of people in frock coats, and after some one had read Lincoln's Gettysburg address he was given a gold shovel and told to go ahead. Fortunately the people didn't stick around and watch him, as they figured out that he might be embarrassed by so many spectators, so he stuck the shovel in the ground and waved good-bye to everyone, and then bent over as if he were going to work. As a matter of fact, he was in a terrible state of mind.

He looked across at the other bank and tried to figure out how far it was. Then he looked behind him and tried to figure out how far that was. He thought that maybe the thing to do was to go and get the bridge made somewhere else, bring it to this spot, and stick one end of it in the hole he had dug and then swing it around until the other end was over the other bank, but that didn't seem practical. So he sat down and began writing some letters he had been meaning to write for months. Then he started throwing shovels full of dirt into the river, hoping against hope that he might get enough of it piled up on the river bottom to make a kind of bridge in itself, but he couldn't even make it show above the surface in one spot.

Just then a man with a rod and a fish basket happened to stroll by and asked him what he was doing.

" You will just laugh when I tell you," said the bridge builder.

" No, I won't, honestly," said the fisherman.

" Then you don't laugh easily," said the bridge builder. " I'm building a bridge."

" And a very smart thing to be doing, too," replied the fisherman. " One never can have too many bridges." Then he added, " You see, I didn't laugh."

This so endeared him to the bridge builder that he offered the stranger a drink, and one thing led to another until they both were sitting on the river bank talking about old songs they used to sing when they were boys.

" Do you remember one that used to go, " Hello ma baby, hello ma lady, hello ma ragtime gal ' ? " asked one.

" ' Send me a kiss by wire, honey, ma heart's on fire ' ? " added the other. " Is that the one you mean ? "

" It sure is," said the other. " And then it went, ' If you refuse me, honey, you lose me, then I'll be left alone '."

" ' So, baby, telephone and tell me I'se your own '," they both sang in unison.

Well, this sort of thing went on for months and months, until they had exhausted all the old songs they used to know and got to making up new ones. The bridge expert forgot entirely what he was there for and the fisherman had never really known, so he had nothing to forget. People used to come over from the town to see how the bridge was coming on and then would tiptoe away again when they saw the two having such a good time. Finally they got someone else to build the bridge, starting from the other side of the river, and what was the surprise of the original bridge expert one day to look up from his game of cribbage with the fisherman and find that they were directly in the way of the vehicular traffic from a brand new bridge. You may be sure that he joined in the laughter, even though the joke was in a way on him. But he saw the fun of the thing, and that is better than any bridge building. What we need in this world is fewer bridges and more fun.

However, the problem of the bridge expert which has just been cited doesn't do much to help those of us who don't understand how a bridge is built. What we want to know is how the second man that the town got went about the job. He evidently knew something about it, for he got the thing done.

I think that it is all that stuff in the air over the river that puzzles me. I can understand the things they build on the banks all right. You go about building those just as you would go about building a house, except, of course, for the windows and front porch. But all those wires and hangings which are suspended from apparently nowhere and yet are strong enough to hold up any number of automobiles and trolley cars that take it into their heads to cross the river. There is something very fishy about those. Who supports them ? I don't like the looks of it, frankly.

Of course, I suppose that if I had gone a little further in mathematics in school I would be a little easier in my mind about bridges. There is evidently something beyond plane geometry which I don't know about and which may hold the key to this mystery. Maybe it's in plane geometry. I missed a couple of days when I had a sore throat, and perhaps those are the days when the geometry class took up bridge building. Or it is quite possible that I actually studied it and didn't absorb it. I would say that my absorption point in mathematics was about .007, and I would not be surprised to find out that I had missed the whole point entirely.

However, even though your engineer has it all worked out mathematically on paper, with figures and digits all over the place, I still don't see how they get those wires up there in the air or how the wires are induced to hold things up. I studied physics and I'm no fool. You can't tell me that all that weight isn't pulling down, and my question is, " Down from what ? "

I don't mean to be nasty about this thing, or narrow-minded. Neither do I incline to the theory of witchcraft—much. There is a man in India, so they tell me, who throws a rope up in the air and then climbs up it, which is evidently the principle of bridge building. But that man in India is supposed to be a fakir, and, according to some theories, the spectators are hypnotised into thinking they see him climb the rope, whereas he is actually not doing it at all. This would be a good explanation of bridges if it were not for the fact that you can't hypnotise a truck into thinking it is crossing a river.

Of course, the old-fashioned covered bridge is easy enough to understand. People could wade right out into those rivers and stick the posts in by hand or at any rate could get planks long enough to reach across. All that was necessary was to get good planks that would rumble. And, by the way, what has become of the old-fashioned rumbling plank ? You never hear planks rumbling to-day as they used to on those old covered bridges. I once spent the night in a farmhouse which I later found out was near a covered bridge. In the middle of the night I heard what I thought was thunder ; so I got up and shut the window. The room got very hot in about half an hour, so, hearing no more thunder, I thought that the storm had passed us by, and got up and opened the window again. In about ten minutes there was another rumble ; this time very loud. With a bound I was out of bed and had the window down in a jiffy. Then came half an hour of stifling again, with a pronounced odour of burning hay from the mattress. I got up and looked out the window. The stars were shining. So up she came again and I went to bed after stepping on both my shoes, which were lying upside down by the bed. This went on at intervals of half an hour all night, until I finally overcame my fear of thunderstorms and decided to let the lightning come right in and get into bed with me if it wanted to, rather than shut the window again. I have already given away the point of this story, so I need hardly say that I found out in the morning that it actually had been thunder that I had heard and that the town on the other side of the mountain had had a bad storm all night. The covered bridge, however, could have been responsible for the rumbling if it had wanted to.

This little anecdote, exciting and amusing as it has been for all of us, I am sure, has drawn us quite a long way from the theme of this treatise, which, you will remember, was, " What Sort of Trickery Goes Into the Building of Bridges ? " I don't happen to know many bridge engineers, so I am unable to say whether they are tricksters as a class. In fact, the only one that I know built a privately owned toll bridge across a river once, and then found that the township ran a free bridge about half a mile down the river around a bend which he hadn't seen before. So he hung his bridge with Japanese lanterns and limited it to rickshas and spent his vacations fishing from it.

But, aside from possibly taking on a job for building a pontoon bridge, which I could do if I had enough boats, I am distinctly not in the market for a bridge contract until some one explains the principle of the thing more clearly to me.

I once read of a man who was caught in a hotel fire and broke open one of those glass cases containing what is known as a " fire axe." Then, as he stood there, axe in hand, watching little curls of smoke coming up through the floor, he tried to figure out what to do with the axe. He could chop a hole in the floor and let more fire up, or he could chop a hole in the wall and make a nice draught. Aside from those two courses of action he seemed to be saddled with an axe and that was all. After waving it weakly around his head once or twice, thinking maybe to frighten the fire away, he just stood there, making imaginary chopping motions, until the firemen came and carried him out still asking, " What do I do with this ? "

Such will be my dilemma when some one puts a shovel in my hand and says : " How about building a bridge ? "

The Sunday Menace

I AM not a gloomy man by nature, nor am I easily depressed. I always say that, no matter how much it looks as if the sun were never going to stop shining and no matter how long the birds carry on their seemingly incessant chatter, there is always a good sleet storm just around the corner and a sniffly head cold in store for those who will only look for it. You can't keep Old Stepmother Nature down for long.

But I frankly see no way out of the problem of Sunday afternoon. For centuries Sunday afternoon has been Old Nell's Curse among the days of the week. Sunday morning may be cheery enough, with its extra cup of coffee and litter of Sunday newspapers, but there is always hanging over it the ominous threat of 3 p.m., when the sun gets around to the back windows and Life stops dead in its tracks. No matter where you are—in China, on the high seas, or in a bird's nest—about 3 o'clock in the afternoon a pall descends over all the world and people everywhere start trying to think of something to do. You might as well try to think of something to do in the death house at Sing Sing, however, because, even if you do it, where does it get you? It is still Sunday afternoon.

The Blue Jeebs begin to drift in along about dessert at Sunday dinner. The last three or four spoonfuls of ice cream somehow lose their flavour and you begin crumbling up your cake instead of eating it. By the time you have finished coffee there is a definite premonition that before long, maybe in 40 or 50 minutes, you will be told some bad news, probably involving the death of several favourite people, maybe even yourself. This feeling gives way to one of resignation. What is there to live for, anyway? At this point, your dessert begins to disagree with you.

On leaving the dining room and wandering aimlessly into the living room (living room indeed; there will be precious little living done in that room this afternoon), everyone begins to yawn. The drifts of Sunday papers on the floor which looked so cozy before dinner now are just depressing reminders of the transitory nature of human life. Uncle Ben makes for the sofa and promptly drops off into an unattractive doze. The children start quarrelling among themselves and finally involve the grownups in what threatens to be a rather nasty brawl.

" Why don't you go out and play ? " someone asks.

" Play what ? " is their retort, and a good one, too.

This brings up the whole question of what to do and there is a half-hearted attempt at thinking on the part of the more vivacious members of the party. Somebody goes to the window and looks out. He goes back to his chair, and somebody else wanders over to another window and looks out there, pressing the nose against the pane and breathing absent-mindedly against the glass. This has practically no effect on the situation.

In an attempt to start conversation, a garrulous one says, " Heigh-ho ! " This falls flat, and there is a long silence while you look through the pile of newspapers to see if you missed anything in the morning's perusal. You even read the ship news and the book advertisements.

" This life of Susan B. Anthony looks as if it might be a pretty good book," you say.

" What makes you think so ? " queries Ed crossly. Ed came out to dinner because he was alone in town, and now wishes he hadn't. He is already thinking up an excuse to get an early train back.

There being no good reason why you think that the life of Susan B. Anthony might be interesting, you say nothing. You didn't really think that it might be interesting, anyway.

A walk is suggested, resulting in groans from the rest of the group. The idea of bridge arouses only two out of the necessary four to anything resembling enthusiasm. The time for the arrival of Bad News is rapidly approaching and by now it is pretty fairly certain to involve death. The sun strikes in through the window and you notice that the green chair needs reupholstering. The rug doesn't look any too good, either. What's the use, though ? There would be no sense in getting a lot of new furniture when everyone is going to be dead before long, anyway.

It is a funny thing about the quality of the sunshine on a Sunday afternoon. On other days it is just sunshine and quite cheery in its middle-class way. But on Sunday afternoon it takes on a penetrating harshness which does nothing but show up the furniture. It doesn't make any difference where you are. You may be hanging around the Busy Bee lunch in Hong Kong or polishing brass on a yacht in the North Sea ; you may be out tramping across the estate of one of the vice-presidents of a big trust company or teaching Indians to read in Arizona. The Sunday afternoon sunlight makes you dissatisfied with everything it hits. It has got to be stopped.

When the automobile came in it looked as if the Sunday afternoon problem was solved. You could climb in at the back door of the old steamer and puff out into the country, where at least you couldn't hear people playing " Narcissus " on the piano several houses away. (People several houses away are always playing " Narcissus " on the piano on Sunday afternoons. If there is one sound that is typical of Sunday afternoon, it is that of a piano being played several houses away.) It is true, of course, that even out in the country, miles away from everything, you could always tell that it was Sunday afternoon by the strange behaviour of the birds, but you could at least pick out an open field and turn somersaults (first taking the small change out of your pockets), or you could run head-on into a large oak, causing insensibility. At least, you could in the early days of automobiling.

But, as soon as everybody got automobiles, the first thing they did naturally was to try to run away from Sunday afternoon, with the result that every country road within a hundred miles of any

I really have no remedy for Sunday afternoons.

city has now taken the place of the old-time county fair, without the pleasure of the cattle and the jam exhibits. To-day the only difference between Sunday afternoon in the city and Sunday afternoon in the country is that, in the country, you don't know the people who are on your lap.

Aside from the unpleasantness of being crowded in with a lot of strangers on a country road and not knowing what to talk about during the long hours while the automobiles are waiting to move ahead, there is the actual danger of an epidemic. Supposing some one took a child out riding in the country on Sunday and while they were jammed in line with hundreds of thousands of other pleasure riders the child came down with tonsilitis. There she would be, a carrier of disease, in contact with at least two-thirds of the population, giving off germs right and left and perhaps starting an epidemic which would sweep the country before the crowds could get back to their homes and gargle. Subways and crowded tenements have long been recognised as breeding grounds for afflictions of the nose and throat. Are country roads on Sunday afternoons to be left entirely without official regulation?

I really have no remedy for Sunday afternoon, at least none that I have any confidence in. The only one that might work would be to rearrange the week in your own mind so that Sunday afternoon falls on Saturday. Now, Saturday afternoon is as cheery as Sunday afternoon is depressing. Perhaps we might try taking a day from some week, let us say a Wednesday which wouldn't matter, then Saturday would be Sunday and Sunday would be Monday. This would do away with all that problem of what to do on Sunday afternoon, because there are always plenty of things to do on Saturday. And you would get the benefit of Saturday afternoon sunshine, which is really delightful. Sunday afternoon sunshine would then wreak its havoc on Monday afternoon and you would be working anyway and might not notice it.

Of course, this system would be complicated unless everybody else would agree to make the same rearrangement in the week, and that might take quite a long time to bring about. If you were making a date for, let us say, Friday morning, you would have to say, " That would be Thursday morning of your week," and perhaps people would get irritated at that. In fact, word might get around that you were a little irresponsible and your business might drop off. Personally, a little slump in business would not be too great a price for me to pay for having Sunday fall on Saturday, but I don't suppose that I could sell the idea to many of you money-mad Americans. I may have to be a lone pioneer in the thing and perhaps be jeered at as Fulton was jeered at. All right, go ahead and jeer.

But, until the thing is in good running order, there will have to be some suggestions as to what to do on Sunday afternoon as we have it now. I can do no more than hint at them, but if there is one among them which appeals to you in outline, I will be glad to take it up with you in more detail.

First, I would suggest setting fire to the house along about 1.30 p.m. If the fire were nursed along, it would cause sufficient excitement to make you forget what day it was, at least until it was time to turn on the lights for the evening. Or you might go down into the cellar right after dinner and take the furnace apart, promising yourself to have it put together again by supper time. Here, at least, the sunlight couldn't get at you. Or you could rent a diver's suit and go to the nearest body of water and spend the afternoon tottering about under the surface, picking sea anemone and old bits of wreckage.

The method which I myself have tried with considerable success and little expense, however, is to buy a small quantity of veronal at the nearest druggist's, put it slyly in my coffee on Saturday night, and then bundle off to bed. When you wake up on Monday morning you may not feel crisp, but Sunday will be over.

And that, I take it, is what we are after.

Ask Me a Question

PROFESSORS in our universities are getting awfully nosey of late. They are always asking questions or sending out questionnaires inquiring into your private life. I can remember the day when all that a professor was supposed to do was to mark " C minus " on students' examination papers and then go home to tea. Nowadays they seem to feel that they must know just how much we (outside the university) eat, what we do with our spare time, and how we like our eggs. I, for one, am inclined not to tell any more. I already have filled in enough stuff on questionnaires to get myself divorced or thrown into jail.

A particularly searching series of questions has just come from an upstate university trying to find out about my sleeping habits. The director of the psychological laboratory wants to know a lot of things which, if I were to give them out, would practically put me in the position of sleeping in John Wanamaker's window. I would have no more privacy than Irvin Cobb.

The first question is a simple one : " How many hours do you sleep each night, on the average ? "

Well, professor, that would be hard to say. I might add " and what's it to you ? " but I suppose there must be some reason for wanting to know. I can't imagine any subject of less general interest than the number of hours I sleep each night on the average. No one has ever given a darn before, and I must say that I am rather touched at this sudden display of interest on the part of a stranger. Perhaps if I were to tell him that I hardly sleep at all he would come down and read to me.

But I would like to bet that the professor gets a raft of answers. If there is one thing that people like to talk about it is their sleeping habits. Just get a group started telling how much or how little they sleep each night and you will get a series of personal anecdotes which will put the most restless member of the party to sleep in no time.

" Well, it's a funny thing about me," one will say. " I get to bed, we'll say, at 11.30, and I go to sleep the minute my head hits the pillow and sleep right through until 7.30.

He will be interrupted at this point by some one who insists on having it known that the night before he heard the clock strike 2, 3 and 4. (People always seem to take a great deal of pride in having heard the clock strike 2, 3 and 4. You will seldom find one who admits having slept soundly all through the night. Just as a man will never admit that the suit he has on is new, so is he loath to confess that he is a good sleeper. I don't understand it, but, as I am getting pretty old now, I don't much care.)

You will be lucky if, in an experience meeting of this kind, you don't start some one off telling the dream he had a few nights ago.

"It was the darndest thing," some one will say, as the rest pay no attention, but try to think up dreams they themselves have had recently, " it was the darndest thing. I seemed to be in a sort of big hall, only it wasn't exactly a hall either ; it was more of a rink or schoolhouse. It seemed that Harry was there and all of a sudden instead of Harry it was Lindbergh. Well, so we all were going to a football game or something and I had on my old grey suit, except that it had wheels on it——"

By this time everybody is engaged in lighting cigarettes or looking at newspapers or even talking to someone else in a low tone of voice and the narrator of the dream has practically no one to listen to him except the unfortunate who happens to be sitting next. But he doesn't seem to care and goes right on, until he has finished. There is a polite murmur of "What had you been eating ? " or " That certainly was a corker," and then someone else starts. The professor who sent this questionnaire will have to watch out for this sort of thing or he will be swamped.

The whole list is just a temptation to garrulousness. Question No. 3, for example, is likely to get people started on an hour's personal disclosure. " Do you notice ill effects the day after sleeping on a train ? " is the way it is worded.

Well, now take me for example. I'm glad you asked that, professor. I do notice ill effects the day after sleeping on a train. I notice, in the first place, that I haven't got my underthings buttoned correctly.

Dressing in a Pullman berth is, at best, a temporary form of arraying oneself, but if I happen to have to go right from the train to my engagement without going first to a hotel and doing the whole thing over again, I find, during the day, that I have buttoned the top button of my running drawers into the bottom buttonhole of my waistcoat and that one whole side of my shirt is clamped, by some mysterious process, half way up my back. This, as the day wears on, exerts a pull on the parts affected until there is grave danger of the whole body becoming twisted to the right, or left, as the case

may be. This, in turn, leads to an awkward gait in walking and is likely to cause comment. Of course, if it is a strange town, people may think that you walk that way naturally and, out of politeness, say nothing about it, but among friends you are pretty sure to be accused of affectation or even worse.

Another ill effect, professor, which I feel after having slept on a Pullman (leaving aside the inevitable cold in the head acquired from sleeping with a light brown blanket piled high on one hip), is the strange appearance I present when I take my hat off.

As I am usually the last man in the washroom, I am constantly being harried by the porter, who keeps coming to the door and telling me that the train is pulling out into the yards in three minutes. (It is always three minutes, never less and never, by any chance, more.) Now, with this unpleasant threat hanging over me, I am in no state of mind to make my customary exquisite toilet. I brush my teeth and possibly shave one-half of my face, but almost invariably forget to brush my hair. It is all right going through the station with my hat on, but later in the day, when I come to my business appointments, I notice that I am the object of considerable curious attention from people who do not know me, owing to my hair standing on end during an entire conference or even a luncheon. It is usually laid to my being a writer and of an artistic temperament, but it doesn't help me in a business way.

Now you will see what you got yourself into by merely asking me that one question, professor. I could go on like this for hours, telling about the ill effects I feel the day after sleeping in a Pullman, but maybe you aren't interested any longer. I am afraid I have bored you already.

The next question, however, is likely to start me off again. "Do you really sleep through the night without awakening?"

It is funny that you should have asked that. I was just about to tell you anyway. Some nights I do, and some nights I don't. I can't be any more explicit than that.

When my little boys were small, I really can't say that I did. Not that they really meant to be mean about it, or did it deliberately, but, as I look back on it, it seems that there was always something. A glass of water was usually the ostensible excuse, but a great many times it turned out to be just a desire on their part to be chummy and have someone to cry with. I would say that, during the infancy of my bairn, my average was something like 10 complete arisings from bed during the night and 15 incomplete ones. By "incomplete" I mean those little starts out of a sound sleep, where one leg is thrust out from under the bedclothes while one waits to see if maybe the disturbance will not die down of its own accord.

These abortive arisings are really just as disturbing to the sleep as the complete ones, and should count as much in any scientific survey. (I do not want to convey the impression that I did all the hopping up during the night. The mother of the boys did her share, but it was a good two-man job on which turns had to be taken.

It also depended a lot on which one could the better simulate sleep at the time of the alarm.)

Now that the boys are old enough to get up and get Daddy water when he wants it, things are a little different, but I find that the amount of undisturbed sleep that I get in one night's rest is dependent on so many outside factors that it is almost impossible to make up any statistics on the subject. A great deal of it depends on the neighbours and how much fun they happen to be having. Then there is the question of what tunes I've heard during the day. One good, monotonous tune firmly imbedded in my consciousness will make going to bed just a matter of form.

Two nights ago I retired early for a good rest (my first in nine years), but unfortunately spent seven out of my possible eight hours trying to get " What Is This Thing Called Love ? " out of my mind. If I had only known some more of the words it wouldn't have been quite so bad, but one can't go on, hour after hour, mentally singing " What is this thing called love—what is this thing called love— what is this thing called love," without suffering some sort of nervous breakdown. It would have been much better for me to have been walking the streets than lying there in bed, plugging a song for nobody in particular.

It is this sort of thing which makes it difficult to answer Question No. 4. One night I am one way ; the next night I am another way.

The only means that I can think of for the professor to employ to get an accurate check-up on my sleeping habits would be for him to come down to my place and sleep on an army cot at the foot of my bed himself. He would have to bring his own blankets, though, as I have hardly enough for myself as it is.

More Songs for Meller

AS Senorita Raquel Meller sings entirely in Spanish, it is again explained, the management prints little synopses of the songs on the programme, telling what each is all about and why she is behaving the way she is. They make delightful reading during those periods when Senorita Meller is changing mantillas, and, in case she should run out of songs before she runs out of mantillas, we offer a few new synopses for her repertoire.

(1) ¿ Voy Bien ?
(AM I GOING IN THE RIGHT DIRECTION ?)

When the acorns begin dropping in Spain there is an old legend that for every acorn which drops there is a baby born in Valencia. This is so silly that no one pays any attention to it now, not even the gamekeeper's daughter, who would pay attention to anything.

She goes from house to house, ringing doorbells and then running away. She hopes that some day she will ring the right doorbell and will trip and fall, so that Prince Charming will catch her. So far, no one has even come to the door. Poor Pepita! if that is her name.

(2) Camisetas de Flanela
(flannel vests)

Princess Rosamonda goes nightly to the Puerta del Sol to see if the early morning edition of the papers is out yet. If it isn't she hangs around humming to herself. If it is, she hangs around humming just the same. One night she encounters a young matador who is returning from dancing school. The finches are singing and there is Love in the air. Princess Rosamonda ends up in the Police Station.

(3) La Guia
(the time-table)

It is the day of the bull fight in Madrid. Everyone is cock-eyed. The bull has slipped out by the back entrance to the arena and has gone home, disgusted. Nobody notices that the bull has gone except Nina, a peasant girl who has come to town that day to sell her father. She looks with horror at the place in the Royal Box where the bull ought to be sitting and sees there instead her algebra teacher whom she had told that she was staying at home on account of a sick headache. You can imagine her feelings!

(4) No Puedo Comer Eso
(i can not eat that!)

A merry song of the Alhambra—of the Alhambra in the moonlight—of a girl who danced over the wall and sprained her ankle. Lititia is the ward of grouchy old Pampino, President of the First National Banco. She has never been allowed further away than the edge of the piazza because she teases people so. Her lover has come to see her and finds that she is fast asleep. He considers that for once he has the breaks, and tiptoes away without waking her up. Along about eleven o'clock she awakes, and is sore as all get-out.

(5) La Lavandera
(the laundryman)

A coquette, pretending to be very angry, bites off the hand of her lover up to the wrist. Ah, naughty Cirinda! Such antics! However does she think she can do her lessons if she gives up all her time to love-making? But Cirinda does not care. Heedless, heedless Cirinda!

(6) Abra Vd. Esa Ventana
(open that window)

The lament of a mother whose oldest son is too young to vote. She walks the streets singing: "My son can not vote! My son is not old enough!" There seems to be nothing that can be done about it.

Museum Feet

A Complaint Contracted by Over-zealous Parents

THERE is one big danger in the approach of Autumn, and that is that the snappy weather may excite us into making plans for doing things we ought to have done long ago. Those of us who are parents are likely to decide that we haven't been paying enough attention to the children, that we ought to take them out more to places of interest and instruction. More of a pal than a father, is what we feel we ought to be, and yet withal an instructor, steering them into enlightening byways and taking them on educational trips to fisheries and jute manufactories, etc.

Now this is just a manifestation of Fall Fever, and will die down, so don't give in to it. Let the children educate themselves. You haven't done such a swell job with yourself that you should undertake to show someone else how to do it. And, above all, never take the kiddies to a natural history museum. Taking them to a natural history museum is one of the things a parent first feels coming on when the crisp Autumn days send the blood tingling through his veins, and it's one of the last things he should do.

I, myself, in a burst of parental obligation last Fall, decided to take the boys through the Smithsonian Institution in Washington. I would have picked a *bigger* place if there had been one in the country, but the Smithsonian was the biggest I could get. As a result I contracted a bad case of what is known in medical circles as " Smithsonian feet," that is, a complete paralysis of the feet from the ankles down, due to standing on first one foot and then the other in front of exhibition cases and walking miles upon miles up and down the tessellated corridors of the museum. The boys suffered no ill effects from the trip at all.

The sad thing about a trip through a museum with the children is that you start out with so much vigour and zip. On entering the main entrance lobby, you call back Herbert who takes a running slide across the smooth floor, and tell him that he must stay close to Daddy and that Daddy will show him everything and explain everything. And what a sap that makes Daddy before the day is done!

In your care not to miss anything, you stop and examine carefully the very first tablet in the entrance lobby, deciding to work to the left and look at everything on the left side of the building, and then take up the right side.

" Look, boys," you say, " it says here that this building was built by the Natural History Society of America in 1876—Oh, well, I guess that isn't very important." And you ask the attendant at the door which is the most satisfactory way to see the museum, a foolish question at best. He tells you to begin with the Glacier Hall over there at the right. This upsets your plans a little, but

Arthur has by this time appeared several miles down the building.

what difference does it make whether you see the right or left side first?

"Come on, boys," you call to both of them who are now sliding back and forth on the floor. "Here is the room where the glaciers are. Come on and look at the glaciers."

The boys by this time are very hot and sweaty, and probably less interested in glaciers than in anything else in the world. You, yourself, find nothing particularly thrilling about the rocks which are lined up for inspection in the room as you enter. However, it is a pretty important thing, this matter of glacial deposits, and both you and the boys would be better off for knowing a little something about them.

H

"Look, Herbert," you say. "Look, Arthur! See here where the glacier went right over this rock and left these big marks."

But Herbert is already in the next hall, which for some mysterious reason is devoted to stuffed rats demonstrating the Malthusian Doctrine—and Arthur has disappeared entirely.

"Where's Arthur, Herbert?" you yell.

"Look, Daddy," replies Herbert from across the hall. "Come here quick! Quick, Daddy!" There evidently is some danger that the stuffed rats are going to get away before you arrive, and you have to run to hush Herbert up, although you had much rather not look at stuffed rats, Malthusian Doctrine or no Malthusian Doctrine.

Arthur has, by this time, appeared several miles down the building in the Early American Indian Room and screams:

"Come quick, Daddy! Look! Indians!"

So you and Herbert set off on a dog trot to the Early American Indian Room.

"You boys *must not* yell so in here," you warn. "And stop running, Arthur! We've got all day (God forbid!)."

"Where did these Indians live, Daddy?" asks Herbert.

"Oh, around Massachusetts," you explain. "They fought the Pilgrims."

"It says here they lived in Arizona," reads Arthur. (Whoever taught that boy to read, anyway?)

"Well, Arizona *too*," you crawl. "They lived all over."

"What are these, Daddy?"

"Those? Those are hatchet heads. They used them for heads to their hatchets."

"It says here they are flint stones that they struck fire on."

"Flint stones, eh? Well, they're funny-looking flint stones. They must have used them for hatchet heads, too."

"What did they use these for, Daddy?"

"If you can read so well, why don't you read what it says and not ask me so much? Where's Herbert?"

Herbert is now on the point of pushing over a little case of Etruscan bowls in an attempt to get at the figure of a Bœotian horse in the case behind it.

"Here, Herbert, don't push that like that! Do you want to break it?"

"Yes," replies Herbert, giving you a short answer.

"Well, we'll go right home if you are going to act that way." (Here a good idea strikes you: Why *not* go right straight home and blame it on Herbert?)

The first evidences of "Smithsonian feet" are beginning to make themselves felt. You try walking on your ankles to favour the soles of your feet, but that doesn't help. And you haven't even struck the second floor yet.

By actual count, the word "look" has been called out eighty-two times, and each time you have looked. Forty-three questions have been asked, forty of which you have answered incorrectly and thirty-four of which you have been caught answering incorrectly. It is high time that you did go home.

But the boys are just beginning. They spot another room at the end of the wing and rush to it. You trail after them, all your old fire gone. It turns out to be Glacier Hall again.

You trail after them, all the old fire gone.

"We've been in here before," you say, hoping that this will discourage them. "There's the door to the street over there. How about going home and coming again to-morrow?"

This suggestion is not even heard, for the boys are on their way up the big flight of stairs leading to the second floor. If you can make half the flight you will be doing well. By the time you reach the first landing, you are in a state of collapse.

"Look, Daddy!" you hear the little voices calling from above. "Come quick, Daddy! Skeletons!"

And skeletons they are, sure enough. Mastodon skeletons. Herbert, turning the corner hurriedly, comes suddenly on one and is thrown into a panic. Not a bad idea! Perhaps they might both be frightened into wanting to go home. But Nature herself comes to your rescue. At the end of the mastodon room Herbert comes and whispers to you.

"I don't know," you reply hopefully. "Perhaps we had better go home."

"No," screams Herbert. "I want to stay here."

"Well, come along with me then, and we'll see if we can find it.

Come on, Arthur. Come with Herbert and Daddy."

So, on the pretext of locating the section of the building in question you lead the boys downstairs and out the back way.

"Over here, I guess," you say. "No, I guess over there."

By this time, you are at the street and within hailing distance of a taxi. It is but the work of a minute to hit Herbert over the head until he is quiet and to yank Arthur into the cab along with you.

"Drive quickly to 468 Elm Avenue," you say to the driver.

That would be your home address.

The Treasurer's Report

Author's Note

ABOUT eight years ago (eight, to be exact) I was made a member of a committee to plan a little Sunday night entertainment for some newspapermen who wanted to act. The committee was supposed to meet at a certain time, each member with some suggestions for sketches or song numbers. (In order to get out of this morass of pussy-footing which I have got myself into, I will come right out and say that the "certain time". at which the committee was to meet was 8 p.m. on Sunday night.) At 7.15 p.m. I suddenly realised that I had no suggestions to offer for the entertainment.

As all the other members of the committee were conscientious workers, I felt considerably abashed. But as they were also charming and indulgent fellows, I knew that they would take my dereliction in good part if I could only take their minds off the business of the meeting and possibly put them in good humour with a comical story or a card trick. So, on the way up in the taxi, I decided to make believe, when they called on me for my contribution, that I had misunderstood the purpose of the committee meeting and had come prepared to account for the year's expenditures. These I jotted down on the back of an old shirt.

As is always the case with such elaborate trickery, my plan to escape censure by diverting the minds of the committee fell flat. They listened to my temporising report and voted me a droll chap, but then they said : "And now what are your suggestions for the entertainment ? " As I had to confess that I had none, it was agreed that, *faute de mieux*, I should elaborate the report I had just offered and perhaps acquire some skill in its delivery, and give that as my share of the Sunday night entertainment. At this moment my entire life changed its course.

I guess that no one ever got so sick of a thing as I, and all my friends, have grown of this Treasurer's Report. I did it every night and two matinees a week for nine months in the Third Music Box

Revue. Following that, I did it for ten weeks in vaudeville around the country, I did it at banquets and teas, at friends' houses and in my own house, and finally went to Hollywood and made a talking movie of it. In fact, I have inflicted it on the public in every conceivable way except over the radio and dropping it from airplanes. But I have never written it. I have been able to throw myself into a sort of trance while delivering it, so that the horrible monotony of the thing made no impression on my nerve cells, but to sit down and put the threadbare words on paper has always seemed just a little too much to bear.

I am writing it out now more as a release than anything else. Perhaps, in accordance with Freudian theories, if I rid myself of this thing which has been skulking in the back of my mind for eight years, I shall be a normal man again. No one has to read it. I hope that no one does, for it doesn't read at all well. All I want to do is get it on paper and out of the way. I feel better already, just from having told all this. And please let's never bring the matter up again.

* * *

The report is delivered by the Assistant Treasurer who has been called in to pinch-hit for the regular Treasurer who is ill. He is not a very good public speaker, this assistant, but after a few minutes of confusion is caught up by the spell of his own oratory and is hard to stop.

I shall take but a very few moments of your time this evening, for I realise that you would much rather be listening to this interesting entertainment than to a dry financial statement . . . but I *am* reminded of a story—which you have probably all of you heard.

It seems that there were these two Irishmen walking down the street when they came to a—oh, I should have said in the first place that the parrot which was hanging out in *front* of the store—or rather belonging to one of these two fellows—the *first* Irishman, that is—was—well, *any*way, this parrot——

(After a slight cogitation, he realises that, for all practical purposes, the story is as good as lost; so he abandons it entirely and, stepping forward, drops his facile, story-telling manner and assumes a quite spurious businesslike air.)

Now, in connection with reading this report, there are one or two points which Dr. Murnie wanted brought up in connection with it, and he has asked me to bring them up in connec—to bring them up.

In the first place, there is the question of the work which we are trying to do up there at our little place at Silver Lake, a work which we feel not only fills a very definite need in the community but also fills a very definite need—er—in the community. I don't think that many members of the Society realise just how big the work is that we are trying to do up there. For instance, I don't think that it is generally known that most of our boys are between the age of fourteen. We feel that, by taking the boy at this age, we can get closer to his real nature—for a boy *has* a very real nature, you may be sure—and bring him into closer touch not only with the school, the parents, and with each other, but also with the town in which they live, the country to whose flag they pay allegiance, and to the—ah—(*trailing off*) town in which they live.

Now the fourth point which Dr. Murnie wanted brought up was that in connection with the installation of the new furnace last Fall. There seems to have been considerable talk going around about this not having been done quite as economically as it might—have—been—done, when, as a matter of fact, the whole thing *was* done just as economically as possible—in fact, even *more* so. I have here a report of the Furnace Committee, showing just how the whole thing was handled from start to finish.

(*Reads from report, with considerable initial difficulty with the stiff covers.*)

Bids were submitted by the following firms of furnace contractors, with a clause stating that if we did not engage a firm to do the work for us we should pay them nothing for submitting the bids. This clause alone saved us a great deal of money.

The following firms, then, submitted bids :

Merkle, Wybigant Co., the Eureka Dust Bin and Shaker Co., The Elite Furnace Shop, and Harris, Birnbauer and Harris. The bid of Merkle, Wybigant being the lowest, Harris Birnbauer were selected to do the job.

(*Here a page is evidently missing from the report, and a hurried search is carried on through all the pages, without result*).

Well, that pretty well clears up that end of the work.

Those of you who contributed so generously last year to the floating hospital have probably wondered what became of the money. I was speaking on this subject only last week at our up-town branch, and, after the meeting, a dear little old lady, dressed all in lavender, came up on the platform, and, laying her hand on my arm, said : " Mr. So-and-So (calling me by name), Mr. So-and-So, what the hell did you do with all the money we gave you last year ? " Well, I just laughed and pushed her off the platform, but it has occurred to the committee that perhaps some of you, like that little old lady, would be interested in knowing the disposition of the funds.

Now, Mr. Rossiter, unfortunately our treasurer—or rather Mr. Rossiter our *treasurer, unfortunately* is confined at his home to-night with a bad head-cold and I have been asked (*he hears someone whispering at him from the wings, but decides to ignore it*) and I have been asked if I would (*the whisperer will not be denied so he goes over to the entrance and receives a brief message, returning beaming and laughing to himself*). Well, the joke seems to be on *me* ! Mr. Rossiter has *pneumonia* !

Following, then, is a summary of the Treasurer's Report :

(*Reads, in a very businesslike manner.*)

During the year 1929—and by that is meant 1928—the Choral Society received the following in donations :

B. L. G.	...	...	...	...	...	...	$500
G. K. M.	...	...	...	...	...	...	500
Lottie and Nellie W.——		...	...	...	...	...	500

In memory of a happy summer at Rye Beach   10

Proceeds of a sale of coats and hats left in the boat-house   14.55

And then' the Junior League gave a performance of
"Pinafore" for the benefit of the Fund, which, unfortunately, resulted in a deficit of $300

Then, from dues and charges 2,354.75

And, following the installation of the new furnace, a
saving in coal amounting to $374.75—which made
Dr. Murnie very happy, you may be sure.

Making a total of receipts amounting to $3,645.75

    This is all, of course, reckoned as of June.

In the matter of expenditures, the Club has not been so fortunate.
There was the unsettled condition of business, and the late Spring,
to contend with, resulting in the following—er—rather discouraging
figures, I am afraid.

Expenditures $23,574.85

Then there was a loss, owing to—several things—of   ...   3,326.70

Car fare 4,452.25

And then, Mrs. Rawlins' expense account, when she
went down to see the work they are doing in Baltimore,
came to $256.50, but I am sure that you will all agree
that it was worth it to find out—er—what they are
doing in Baltimore.

And then, under the general head of Odds and Ends   ...   2,537.50

Making a total disbursement of (*hurriedly*)   ... $416,546.75

or a net deficit of—ah—several thousand dollars.

Now, these figures bring us down only to October. In October
my sister was married, and the house was all torn up, and in the
general confusion we lost track of the figures for May and August.
All those wishing the *approximate* figures for May and August,
however, may obtain them from me in the vestry after the dinner,
where I will be with pledge cards for those of you who wish to
subscribe over and above your annual dues, and I hope that each
and every one of you here to-night will look deep into his heart
and (*archly*) into his pocketbook, and see if he can not find it there
to help us to put this thing over with a bang (*accompanied by a wholly
ineffectual gesture representing a bang*) and to help and make this just
the biggest and best year the Armenians have ever had . . . I thank
you.

    (*Exits, bumping into proscenium.*)

Shakespeare Explained

Carrying on the System of Footnotes to a Silly Extreme

PERICLES

ACT II. SCENE 3

Enter first Lady-in-Waiting (Flourish,[1] Hautboys[2] and[3] torches[4]).

First Lady-in-Waiting—What[5] ho ![6] Where[7] is[8] the[9] music ?[10]

NOTES

1. *Flourish* : The stage direction here is obscure. Clarke claims it should read " flarish," thus changing the meaning of the passage to " flarish " (that is, the King's), but most authorities have agreed that it should remain " flourish," supplying the predicate which is to be flourished. There was at this time a custom in the country-side of England to flourish a mop as a signal to the passing vender of berries, signifying that in that particular household there was a consumer demand for berries, and this may have been meant in this instance. That Shakespeare was cognisant of this custom of flourishing the mop for berries is shown in a similar passage in the second part of King Henry IV, where he has the Third Page enter and say, " Flourish." Cf. also Hamlet, IV, 7 : 4.

2. *Hautboys*, from the French *haut*, meaning " high " and the Eng. *boys*, meaning " boys." The word here is doubtless used in the sense of " high boys," indicating either that Shakespeare intended to convey the idea of spiritual distress on the part of the First Lady-in-Waiting or that he did not. Of this Rolfe says : " Here we have one of the chief indications of Shakespeare's knowledge of human nature, his remarkable insight into the petty foibles of this work-a-day world." Cf. T. N. 4 : 6, " Mine eye hath play'd the painter, and hath stell'd thy beauty's form in table of my heart."

3. *and.* A favourite conjunctive of Shakespeare's in referring to the need for a more adequate navy for England. Tauchnitz claims that it should be pronounced " und," stressing the anti-penult. This interpretation, however, has found disfavour among most commentators because of its limited significance. We find the same conjunctive in A. W. T. E. W. 6 : 7, " Steel-boned, unyielding *and* uncomplying virtue," and here there can be no doubt that Shakespeare meant that if the King should consent to the marriage of his daughter the excuse of Stephano, offered in Act 2, would carry no weight.

4. *Torches.* The interpolation of some foolish player and never the work of Shakespeare (Warb.). The critics of the last century have disputed whether or not this has been misspelled in the original, and should read " trochies " or " troches." This might well be since the introduction of tobacco into England at this time had wrought havoc with the speaking voices of the players, and we might well imagine that at the entrance of the First Lady-in-Waiting

there might be perhaps one of the hautboys mentioned in the preceding passage bearing a box of " troches " or " trognies " for the actors to suck. Of this entrance Clarke remarks : " The noble

Might be one of the hautboys bearing a box of " trognies " for the actors to suck.

mixture of spirited firmness and womanly modesty, fine sense and true humility, clear sagacity and absence of conceit, passionate warmth and sensitive delicacy, generous love and self-diffidence with which Shakespeare has endowed this First Lady-in-Waiting renders her in our eyes one of the most admirable of his female characters." Cf. M. S. N. D. 8 : 9, " That solder'st close impossibilities and mak'st them kiss."

5. *What*—What.

6. *Ho !* In conjunction with the preceding word doubtless means " What ho ! " changed by Clarke to " what hoo ! " In the original MS. it reads " What hi ! " but this has been accredited to the tendency of the time to write " What hi " when " what ho " was meant. Techner alone maintains that it should read " What humpf ! " Cf. Ham. 5 : 0, " High-ho ! "

7. *Where.* The reading of the folio, retained by Johnson, the Cambridge editors and others, but it is not impossible that Shakespeare wrote " why," as Pope and others give it. This would make the passage read " Why the music ? " instead of " Where is the music ? " and would be a much more probable interpretation in view of the music of that time. Cf. George Ade. Fable No. 15, " Why the gunny-sack ? "

8. *is*—is not. That is, would not be.

9. *the.* Cf. Ham. 4 : 6. M. S. N. D. 3 : 5. A. W. T. E. W. 2 : 6.

T. N. 1 : 3 and Macbeth 3 : 1, " that knits up *the* ravelled sleeves of care."

10. *music.* Explained by Malone as " the art of making music " or " music that is made." If it has but one of these meanings we are inclined to think it is the first; and this seems to be favoured by what precedes, " *the* music ! " Cf. M. of V. 4 : 2, " The man that hath no music in himself."

The meaning of the whole passage seems to be that the First Lady-in-Waiting has entered, concomitant with a flourish, hautboys and torches and says, " What ho ! Where is the music ? "

When not in Rome, Why Do As the Romans Did?

THERE is a growing sentiment among sign painters that when a sign or notice is to be put up in a public place it should be written in characters that are at least legible, so that, to quote *The Manchester Guardian* (as everyone seems to do) " He who runs may read."

This does not strike one as being an unseemly pandering to popular favour. The supposition is that the sign is put there to be read, otherwise it would have been turned over to an inmate of the Odd Fellows Home to be engraved on the head of a pin. And what could be a more fair requirement than that it should be readable ?

Advertising, with its billboard message of rustless screens and co-educational turkish baths, has done much to further the good cause, and a glance through the files of newspapers of seventyfive years ago, when the big news story of the day was played up in diamond type easily deciphered in a strong light with the naked eye shows that news printing has not, to use a slang phrase, stood still.

But in the midst of this uniform progress we find a stagnant spot Surrounded by legends that are patent and easy to read and understand, we find the stone-cutter and the architect still putting up tablets and corner-stones, monuments and cornices, with dates disguised in Roman numerals. It is as if it were a game, in which they were saying, " The number we are thinking of is even ; it begins with M ; it has five digits and when they are spread out, end to end, they occupy three feet of space. You have until we count to one hundred to guess what it is."

Roman numerals are all right for a rainy Sunday afternoon or to take a convalescent's mind from his illness, but to put them in a public place, where the reader stands a good chance of being run over by a dray if he spends more than fifty seconds in their perusal, is not in keeping with the efficiency of the age. If for no other reason than the extra space they take, involving more marble, more of the cutter's time and wear and tear on his instruments, not to mention the big overhead, you would think that Roman numerals would have been abolished long ago.

Of course, they can be figured out if you're good at that sort of thing. By working on your cuff and backs of envelopes, you can translate them in no time at all compared to the time taken by a cocoon to change into a butterfly, for instance. All you have to do is remember that " M " stands for either " *millium*," meaning thousand, or for " million." By referring to the context you can tell which is more probable. If, for example, it is a date, you can tell right away that it doesn't mean " million," for there isn't any " million " in our dates. And there is one-seventh or eighth of your number deciphered already. Then " C," of course, stands for " *centum*," which you can translate by working backwards at it, taking such a word as " century " or " per cent." and looking up what they come from, and there you have it! By this time it is hardly the middle of the afternoon, and all you have before you is a combination of X's, I's and an L, the latter standing for " Elevated Railway," and " Liquorice," or, if you cross it with two little horizontal lines, it stands for the English pound, which is equivalent to about four dollars and eighty-odd cents in real money. Simple as sawing through a log.

But it takes time. That's the big trouble with it. You can't do the right thing by the office and go in for Roman numerals, too. And since most of the people who pass such inscriptions are dependent on their own earnings, why not cater to them a bit and let them in on the secret?

Probably the only reason that the people haven't risen up and demanded a reform along these lines is because so few of them really give a hang what the inscription says. If the American Antiquarian Turn-Verein doesn't care about stating in understandable figures the date on which the cornerstone of their building was laid, the average citizen is perfectly willing to let the matter drop right there.

But it would never do to revert to Roman numerals in, say, the arrangement of time-tables. How long would the commuter stand it if he had to mumble to himself for twenty minutes and use up the margins of his newspaper before he could figure out what was the next train after the 5.18? Or this, over the telephone between wife and husband:

" Hello, dear! I think I'll come in town for lunch. What trains can I get?"

" Just a minute—I'll look them up. Hold the wire. . . . Let's see, here's one at XII : LVIII, that's twelve, and L is a thousand and V is five and three I's are three; that makes 12: one thousand . . . that can't be right . . . now XII certainly is twelve, and L . . . what does L stand for? . . . I say, what—does—L—stand—for? . . .

Well, ask Helma. . . . What does she say ? . . . Fifty ? . . . Sure, that makes it come out all right . . . 12.58. . . . What time is it now ? . . . 1 o'clock ? . . . Well, the next one leaves Oakam at I : XLIV . . . . that's . . ." etc.

Batting averages and the standing of teams in the leagues are another department where the introduction of Roman numerals would be suicide for the political party in power at the time. For of all things that are essential to the day's work of the voter, an early enlightenment in the matter of the home team's standing and the numerical progress of the favourite batsman are of primary importance. This information has to be gleaned on the way to work in the morning, and, except for those who come in to work each day from North Philadelphia or the Croton Reservoir, it would be a physical impossibility to figure the tables out and get any of the day's news besides.

CLUB BATTING RECORDS

	Games	At Bat	Runs	B.H.	S.B.	S.H.	Aver.
Detroit	CLII	MMMMMXXCIX	DCLIII	MCCCXXXIII	CLXVIII	CC	CCLXII
Chicago	CLI	MMMMCMXL	DLXXI	MCCXLVI	CLXXIX	CCXXI	CCLII
Cleveland	CLII	MMMMCMXXXVII	DCXIX	MCCXXXI	CL	CCXXI	CCXLIX
Boston	CLI	MMMMDCCCLXXIV	DXXXIV	MCXCI	CXXXVI	CCXXV	CCXLV
New York	CL	MMMMCMLXXXVII	DLIV	MCCXXX	CLXXV	CLXV	CCXLVII
Washington	CLIII	MMMMCMXXVIII	DV	MCXC	CLXIII	CLXV	CCXDI
St. Louis	CLV	MMMMMLXV	DLXXIV	MCCXXI	CCVII	CLXII	CCXLI
Philadelphia	CXLIX	MMMMDCCCXXVI	CCCCXVI	MCXLIII	CXLIII	CLV	CCXXXVII

You can't do right by the office and go in for roman numerals too

On matters such as these the proletariat would have protested the Roman numeral long ago. If they are willing to let its reactionary use on tablets and monuments stand it is because of their indifference to influences which do not directly affect their pocket books. But if it could be put up to them in a powerful cartoon, showing the Architect and the Stone-Cutter dressed in frock coats and silk hats, with their pockets full of money, stepping on the Common People so that he cannot see what is written on the tablet behind them, then perhaps the public would realise how they are being imposed on.

For that there is an organised movement among architects and stone-cutters to keep these things from the citizenry there can no longer be any doubt. It is not only a matter of the Roman numerals. How about the use of the " V " when " U " should be used ? You will always see it in inscriptions. " SVMNER BVILDING " is one of the least offensive. Perhaps the excuse is that " V " is more adapted to stone-lettering. Then why not carry this principle out further ? Why not use the letter H when S is meant ? Or substitute K for B ? If the idea is to deceive, and to make it easier for the stone-cutter, a pleasing effect could be got from the inscription, " Erected in 1897 by the Society of Arts and Grafts," by making it read : " EKEATEW IZ MXIXLXIXLXXII LY THE XNLIEZY OF AEXA ZNL ELAFTX." There you have letters that are all adapted to stone-cutting ; they look well together, and they are, *in toto*, as intelligible as most inscriptions.

A Vanishing Art

SOMEHOW I have a feeling that, no matter how far out of work I may be, I shall never be able to make my living by putting little ships into glass bottles. There must be some people who do, for one is constantly seeing bottled ships in store windows. I never could quite figure out just what kind of store it was that would feature a ship in a bottle as a window display, but as there is usually an 18th-century highboy and a pair of bellows alongside the bottle, it can't be one of the more essential emporia. I guess that you would just call it a " ship-in-bottle store."

However, the fact that putting little ships into bottles is not a useful trade is not the reason why I would not go in for it. Look at what I am doing now! No, the reason for my eschewing that form of gainful activity is simply that I haven't the slightest idea how it is done. And I doubt if I ever could learn.

I have often tried to figure it out while standing, on a busy day in my own trade, in front of a ship-in-bottle store. Is it possible that the tiny ship is made and rigged and set up and then the glass blown around it? Blowing glass in itself is enough of a mystery to me without having it complicated by having to blow it around a ship. I rather doubt if that is the way the thing is done.

The only other solution is that the bottle is already blown and the ship is made inside the bottle. This, too, sounds implausible. Some sort of man or woman (or very dexterous child) has got to make the ship, and you can't tell me that anyone, no matter how small, can get right inside one of those bottles and build a ship. I may get a funny, vacant look in my eyes once in a while, and I may not be very good at adding up my check stubs, but I'm no fool. Nobody makes those ships from the inside out.

This leaves what? Nothing! Either the ship is made first or the bottle is made first. The hole in the neck of the bottle is not large enough to allow for a full-rigged ship being let down through it. You can tell that at a glance. There is nothing left except for the ponderer to go crazy. I have tried that, too.

1 once tracked a ship-in-bottle putter to his workshop and tried to find out how he worked it. I was spending the summer on the Atlantic coast (sometimes here and sometimes there, mostly a compromise between the two) and in an old Cape Cod antique shop I saw one of the accursed things. I went into the shop and asked the old lady (don't let her know I called her an " old lady," please) who had made it. She, with that old New England cordiality which has made that section of the country the flourishing centre it now is, left the room without answering me. But I found out from a customer (a summer resident who came from Wisconsin) that a gentleman who lived in the white house down by the steamship dock had wrought this wonder. So I set out in search of him.

His name was Capt. Whipple and he was 167 years old, although he lied about his age and claimed to be only 160.

"Cap'n," I said (from now on I shall spell the title "Captain," but you must remember that what I really said was "Cap'n"), "Captain, how in (naming a certain flower) do you put those little ships into those bottles?" A fair question, and deserving of a fair answer.

The captain whittled a piece from his calloused thumb and spat reflectively. "Wal," he said (from now on I shall spell the words as they should be spelled, without reference to the Cape Cod pronunciation), "Well, it's a long story."

Going back to my hotel and getting a chair, I drew it up beside the old gentleman, all attention.

"Shoot, kid!" I said.

The seafaring man took the stub of a pencil and began figuring on the back of the original of a letter from Thomas Jefferson to Martha Custis (a little scandal which has never come to light, but which, while it lasted, was a peach). Then he looked up at me with his little, watery blue eyes aglint.

"You're from New York, ain't you?" he asked.

I blushed prettily.

"It will cost you just $500 to know," he said. "And, at that, I am cheating myself."

I thought it over. Five hundred dollars to learn how to put a ship in a bottle, when the chances were that I never would be called upon to put anything into a bottle, much less a ship. And even if, at some time or other, I should be faced with the necessity, I could always plead a headache or the fact that I had no ship with me at the moment. So I took an old Revolutionary cradle which was standing nearby and placed it firmly over the old gentleman's head until nothing was visible of him above his shoulders. On this I piled several pewter candlesticks, a spinning wheel, and a portrait of Gen. Howe. This done, I left the ancient mariner and artisan with his secret.

The main trouble, however, with taking up ship-in-bottle putting as a trade (aside from the difficulty of finding out how it is done) would seem to be that it doesn't offer much opportunity for advancement to a young man. You can't get ahead very fast. Suppose you do learn how to do it and serve an apprenticeship to some expert ship-in-bottle putter for five years. You are then promoted to head of the bottling department. What is there left? You are as far as you can go, unless you start in for yourself. And I should imagine that the consumer demand for ships in bottles would be soon exhausted in any one community, with very little turn-over.

One is reminded (and, let us be quite frank about it, when I say "one is reminded" I mean "I am reminded")* of the business troubles of the man who polished the commemorative brass cannon

---

*The author is indebted to Mr. "Terry" McGovern of Cornell University for the following business fable.

126

in Ypsilanti, Mich. (I have always heard that it was Ypsilanti, Mich., but I am willing to retract if it is not true.) It seems that the residents of Ypsilanti, Mich., shortly after the Civil War decided that some sort of monument or *denkmal* should be placed in a public square to remind future generations of Michigan's part in the great struggle. So a large brass commemorative cannon was placed on the common (if there is a common in Ypsilanti) and a veteran of the war was engaged, at a nominal salary, to keep this cannon in good condition. He was to polish it twice a week and see that small boys did not hide in it. Aside from this, his time was his own.

This business routine went on for 25 years. The veteran was faithful at his task of polishing the commemorative brass cannon and its splendor and shining surface were the admiration of everyone who visited Ypsilanti, Mich., during those 25 years, to say nothing of the natives. "The commemorative brass cannon of Ypsilanti, Mich.," became a byword throughout the state for expressing how shiny a commemorative brass cannon could be made.

One evening, during the veteran's 26th year of service, he came home to supper at his usual hour (4.30), but his wife noticed that he was more depressed than was his wont. He hardly touched his food, and sat in moody contemplation of the backs of his polish-stained hands. His wife was worried.

" What is it, Joe ? " she asked. " What is the matter ? "

" Oh, nothing, my dear," said her husband, and turned in a brave attempt to finish his cutlet.

" Come, come," said the companion of his 25 years of labour (he had married immediately on getting the job of polishing the commemorative brass cannon), " I know that something is wrong. You are depressed."

The grey-haired man put down his knife and looked his wife in the eye.

" You're right," he said, as he took her hand in his. " I am depressed. Things haven't been going very well down at the cannon lately."

" You don't mean that you're fired, Joe ! " she said, fearfully.

" No, no ! Never fear about that," was his reply. They couldn't fire me. I know too much. They would be afraid that I might make trouble. But I am discouraged about my work. I don't seem to be getting ahead. For 25 years I have been polishing that cannon and putting everything that I had into making it bright and shiny. I have done my job well—no one can deny that. But recently I have got to thinking. What is it leading to ? Where am I getting ? Where is the future in polishing commemorative brass cannons ? " And the old man broke down and cried.

His wife was silent for a minute. Then she stroked his head and said : " I know, Joe. I have worried a little myself. And I have figured it out this way. In the last 25 years we have saved a little money. I have put aside a dollar here and a dollar there when you didn't know about it. We have quite a tidy little nest egg in the bank now, and here is my suggestion : Let's take that money, buy a cannon, and go into business for ourselves ! "

Such, I should think, would be the problem which would confront every middle-aged man who finds himself, at the age of 55, a putter-in-bottles of little ships. What is the future of such work ? Even if he goes into business for himself like the polisher of the commemorative brass cannon of Ypsilanti, Mich., how can he meet competition ? Of course, he can vary the types of ships he puts into the bottles. The old, square-rigged merchantman having gone out of date, he could put in models of the *Bremen* or destroyers, but, with all this talk of naval reduction going on, dealing in battleships and destroyers is a pretty precarious business.*

England pleads that her navy has been more than an engine of war during the last two centuries, that it has been a career for the finest of her young men. She naturally recoils from any proposition which would eliminate such patrician employment. But what about those unfortunates who find themselves with no models for bottle-putting ? These artisans must either stick to the old clipper ships which their grandfathers put in bottles, or put in battleships which may be, in a few years, against the law. Of course, they could begin putting in models of reapers and binders, or of printing presses, or any of the other thousand-and-two engines of peace, but that really wouldn't be right. It has got to be a ship if the old tradition is to be maintained.

And so, to all young men who are going out into the world to make their living, I would say : " Think twice before you go in for putting little ships in bottles. That is, unless you are planning to spend a lot of your time in jail, where time hangs heavy."

I suppose that I shall get a lot of indignant letters from the trade for issuing this advice. But it comes from the heart.

*This article was obviously written on the eve of that benighted era when nations were busily engaged in sinking not each other's ships, as the custom is to-day, but—oddly enough—their own.—Editor's Note.